Grandma's
cookies, cakes,
pies and sweets
· · · · · ·

The Best of Canada's
East Coast

Grandma's cookies, cakes, pies and sweets
······

The Best of Canada's East Coast

Updated and tested by Alice Burdick
Photography by Callen Singer

FORMAC PUBLISHING COMPANY LIMITED
HALIFAX

Formac Publishing Company Limited recognizes the support of the Province of Nova Scotia through Film and Creative Industries Nova Scotia. We are pleased to work in partnership with the Province of Nova Scotia to develop and promote our creative industries for the benefit of all Nova Scotians. We acknowledge the support of the Canada Council for the Arts which last year invested $157 million to bring the arts to Canadians throughout the country.

Cover design: Tyler Cleroux

Library and Archives Canada Cataloguing in Publication

Title: Grandma's cookies, cakes, pies and sweets : the best of Canada's East Coast / updated and tested by Alice Burdick ; food photography by Callen Singer.

Names: Burdick, Alice, editor. | Singer, Callen, photographer.

Description: Includes index.

Identifiers: Canadiana 20200213016 | ISBN 9781459506398 (softcover)

Subjects: LCSH: Desserts—Nova Scotia. | LCSH: Baking—Nova Scotia. | LCGFT: Cookbooks.

Classification: LCC TX773 .G73 2020 | DDC 641.86—dc23

Formac Publishing Company Limited
5502 Atlantic Street
Halifax, Nova Scotia, Canada
B3H 1G4
www.formac.ca

Printed and bound in Canada.

Acknowledgements

Thanks to Mary Ann Feeney and Madonna Boland for preparing all the recipes photographed in this collection and to Callen Singer for taking the beautiful photographs. Thanks to Kara Turner and Cecilia Stuart for styling during the photo shoot, and to Tyler Cleroux for the art direction. Thanks to Hailey Thomson for the use of her fabulous kitchen and her wonderful collection of vintage props. Her house has the most incredible light. Thank you to Mrs. Florence M. Hilchey for collecting the original recipes in the 1960s and for helping to preserve Nova Scotia's heirloom recipes for future generations. Many thanks to local food producers for sustaining a robust local food economy, with both a respect for tradition and innovation for the future. And, finally, thank you to Hazel and Arthur for being the best taste testers a mother could ask for!

—AB

Contents

INTRODUCTION | 7

COOKIES | 9

CAKES | 25

PIES | 51

DESSERTS | 83

CANDIES | 115

SWEET SAUCES | 121

INDEX | 126

INTRODUCTION

"[May] thy life be as sweet, and its last sunset sky
Golden-tinted and fair, as thy own pumpkin pie!"
— from *The Pumpkin* by John Greenleaf Whittier (1807-1892)

One of the main threads that tie generations together is food. Recipes handed down through a family are a form of time travel — you can imagine a great-great-grandmother tasting the very same flavours as you eat a forkful of home-baked apple pie. The recipes in this collection were originally published in 1967 in *A Treasury of Nova Scotia Heirloom Recipes* — a centennial project of Nova Scotia's Department of Agriculture and Marketing. They were compiled by Mrs. Florence M. Hilchey, supervisor of Home Economics for the department, and were collected from books dating back as far as the 1870s (including the first Canadian cookbook to be printed in Canada, *The Home Cook Book*, from 1877). Many other recipes were supplied by Mrs. Hilchey's mother and other relatives, borrowed from old family cookbooks, scribblers and notebooks.

I've revised, updated and tested all the recipes in this collection, but their essence and time-honoured traditions remain. The original recipe names were often blunt and sometimes unpalatable — so I've updated them to better reflect their flavours and ingredients. While they are all relatively simple recipes, they are packed with a zesty natural sweetness from their featured dried fruit or fresh berries.

Treasured family recipes are a combination of intuition and experience, and you can really see that with older, heirloom recipes, where often whole steps aren't mentioned. There's an assumption that the person reading the recipes is using them as a guide, but already knows the steps. When updating the recipes, I often had to add ingredients, steps and tips that had been left out — the modifications that are made over time, passed on through shared experiences, but aren't written down.

I had the sense with so many of these recipes that they'd been used by generations of families, and minor modifications had been incorporated over the years. I grew up with a mother who cherished our family's recipes. I made many meals with her, and especially treasure the times when we baked together. I was lucky that she assembled all the handwritten recipes and notes into a family cookbook that she called *The Cooking of Joy*, named after my Grandma Joy. This connection with the past is a key element of using traditional recipes, especially the aromas and flavours that we associate with our grandmas' kitchens.

There is something special about the way a fresh-baked cookie or a hot-from-the-oven pie can immediately provide a sense of comfort. When there is a connection to previous generations who made that same sweet, and when it is made of local ingredients, it is especially satisfying. Nova Scotian desserts are an interesting mix of French, British and Northern European origins, but there are also distinctly Indigenous contributions, particularly when it comes to the use of fresh wild fruit and berries, squash and maple syrup.

Every new wave of immigration has brought with it traditional recipes that have been adapted to suit the conditions and ingredients available, making for an interesting and varied cuisine. The French influence is noticeable in the Cheticamp and Isle Madame districts of Cape Breton Island and in the counties of Digby and Yarmouth. Cape Breton Island and Pictou County are centres of Scottish tradition, while Lunenburg County on the South Shore is the nucleus of German culture. The result is a delicious range and combination of flavours firmly rooted in the past but just as fresh and tasty for today's home bakers and all those we feed.

Let the aromas of these baked goods, featuring such traditional ingredients as molasses, raisins, oats, blueberries, cranberries and apples, transport you back into your grandma's kitchen!

Alice Burdick, Mahone Bay, February 2020

BOULARDERIE
ACADIAN COOKIE

Boularderie Island is in Cape Breton on the Bras d'Or Lakes, not that far from Louisbourg. It's been known as Boularderie Island since the early 1700s, when Louis-Simon le Poupet de la Boularderie, a naval officer, was granted the area as a concession from the king of France. This is a thick cookie that is typical of the Acadian style, showcasing the warmth of the spices and molasses.

INGREDIENTS

½ cup (125 mL) butter
1 cup (250 mL) molasses
1 tsp (5 mL) baking soda
1 egg, beaten
2 ½ cups (625 mL) all-purpose flour
1 tsp (5 mL) ground cinnamon
1 tsp (5 mL) ground ginger
½ tsp (2.5 mL) ground allspice
½ tsp (2.5 mL) ground cloves
Pinch of salt

METHOD

Preheat oven to 400°F (200°C). Line a baking sheet with parchment paper and set aside.

In a large heavy pot, melt the butter and molasses together on medium-low, then raise heat to high and bring to a boil. Remove from heat, add the baking soda and then let the mixture cool. Beat in the egg, and add the flour, cinnamon, ginger, allspice, cloves and salt.

Turn the dough out onto a floured surface, then roll it out to a thickness of ½ in (12 mm) and cut into squares.

Place cookies on the baking sheet and bake for 15 to 20 minutes.

Yield: 3 dozen cookies

FAT ARCHIES

{ *Molasses was an early kitchen staple in the Maritimes due to trade between the colonies and Great Britain. Wood was shipped out in the form of timber or as sailing vessels, and molasses would return from sugar plantations in the Caribbean. On Cape Breton Island, Archie (short for Archibald) was a popular name, and that's the genesis for the name of these popular thick cookies. A sturdy companion to a hot cuppa.* }

INGREDIENTS

½ cup (125 mL) butter
½ cup (125 mL) granulated sugar
½ cup (125 mL) brown sugar, packed
1 egg, lightly beaten
½ cup (125 mL) molasses
2 tsp (10 mL) baking soda
½ cup (125 mL) boiling water
2 ½ cups (625 mL) all-purpose flour
1 tsp (5 mL) ground ginger
½ tsp (2.5 mL) ground cinnamon
½ tsp (2.5 mL) ground nutmeg
½ tsp (2.5 mL) salt

METHOD

Preheat oven to 400°F (200°C). Line baking sheets with parchment paper and set aside.

In a large bowl, cream the butter, then add the granulated sugar and brown sugar and blend well. Add the egg to the butter mixture and beat well, then add in the molasses.

In a small bowl, dissolve the baking soda in the boiling water, then add to the butter mixture.

In a medium bowl, sift together the flour, ginger, cinnamon, nutmeg and salt. Add the sifted dry ingredients to the butter mixture, stirring quickly until you achieve a smooth dough.

Pat the dough into a round, wrap in plastic wrap, then refrigerate for at least two hours.

When ready to make the cookies, remove the dough from the refrigerator and let it come to room temperature, around half an hour.

Turn the dough out onto a floured surface, then roll it out to a thickness of ¾ in (20 mm) and cut with 2-in (5-cm) cookie cutter.

Place cookies on the baking sheets and bake for 15 to 20 minutes.

Yield: 3 dozen cookies

CAPE BRETON
LONG JOHNS

{ *This is a very simple cookie, with very few ingredients and molasses as the predominant flavour. There's a story behind the name: an older gentleman compared the experience of eating a hot molasses cookie with the comfort and warmth of a cozy pair of long johns underwear. It would have been relatively inexpensive to make these cookies in Mrs. Hilchey's day, given the lack of spices, so a good everyday cookie. Keep these cookies crisp by storing them in an airtight container once they are completely cool!* }

INGREDIENTS

2 cups (500 mL) molasses
1 tbsp + 1 tsp (20 mL) baking soda
1 tsp (5 mL) salt
4 cups (1 L) all-purpose flour

METHOD

Preheat oven to 350°F (180°C). Line a baking sheet with parchment paper and set aside.

In a bowl, whisk together the molasses and baking soda until light and frothy. In another bowl, sift together the salt and flour, then stir briskly into the molasses mixture.

Turn the dough out onto a floured surface, then roll it out to a thickness of ¼ in (5 mm) and cut into strips.

Score the cookies lightly with a fork, then place on the baking sheet and bake for 15 to 20 minutes.

Yield: 4 dozen cookies

MARGAREE
MOLASSES COOKIES

The Margaree Valley, on the Cabot Trail in Cape Breton, traditionally favoured this sort of cookie, which resembles a ginger snap — thinner than the previous cookies. The flavour of the molasses is still very apparent, but it is less predominant than the other molasses cookies in this collection.

INGREDIENTS

½ cup (125 mL) butter
½ cup (125 mL) granulated sugar
½ cup (125 mL) molasses
1 egg
2 ¼ cups (550 mL) all-purpose flour
1 tsp (5 mL) ground ginger
1 tsp (5 mL) ground cinnamon
½ tsp (2.5 mL) salt
½ tsp (2.5 mL) ground cloves
½ tsp (2.5 mL) ground allspice
6 tbsp (90 mL) cold water
2 tsp (10 mL) baking soda
2 tsp (10 mL) hot water
1 cup (250 mL) raisins (optional)

METHOD

Preheat oven to 400°F (200°C). Line a baking sheet with parchment paper and set aside.

In a bowl, cream the butter and sugar together well, then stir in the molasses. Add the egg to this mixture, and beat it together well.

In another bowl, sift together the flour, ginger, cinnamon, salt, cloves and allspice. Beat the flour mixture into the butter and sugar mixture, then mix in the cold water. Add raisins, if desired, at this point.

In a small bowl, whisk together the baking soda and hot water, then mix well into the dough.

Drop teaspoons of the dough onto the baking sheet, and bake for 10 to 15 minutes.

Yield: 4 dozen cookies

MOLASSES
CRISPS

The original source for this recipe notes that "this recipe is more than 100 years old," so it's even older than that now! This is an aromatic cookie, and the combination of baking soda and vinegar predates the use of baking powder. It's a delightfully crisp, thin, snap-style cookie, with the caramel quality of the molasses boosted by the brown sugar.

INGREDIENTS

1 cup (250 mL) molasses
1 tbsp (15 mL) baking soda
1 tbsp (15 mL) white vinegar
1 cup (250 mL) butter
1 cup (250 mL) brown sugar, packed
1 egg, beaten
4 cups (1 L) all-purpose flour
1 tsp (5 mL) ground ginger
1 tsp (5 mL) ground cloves
1 tsp (5 mL) salt

METHOD

Preheat oven to 350°F (180°C). Line a baking sheet with parchment paper and set aside.

In a large pot on medium-high heat, bring the molasses to a boil. Add the baking soda and vinegar to the molasses, blend well together, and let cool.

In a bowl, cream together the butter with the brown sugar, then beat in the egg. Add the molasses mixture to the butter mixture, and mix well.

In another bowl, sift together the flour with the ginger, cloves and salt, then add this to the wet mixture, stirring well.

(If you wish to bake the cookies at a later point, make the dough into rolls, wrap in waxed paper and refrigerate. Slice into thin rounds and bake as needed.)

Turn the dough out onto a lightly floured surface, then roll it out thinly to a thickness of 1/8 in (3 mm) and cut into rounds using 2-in (5-cm) cutter.

Place the cookies on the baking sheet and bake for 10 to 15 minutes.

Yield: 4 dozen cookies

OLD-FASHIONED
SUGAR COOKIES

{ *This is a classic sugar cookie, with a warm, light texture. Nutmeg was a highly valued spice from the early years of trade onward, and a perfect complement to the toasty butter and sugar flavour of these cookies. These are very pretty alongside some molasses cookies and other sweets on a Christmas dessert plate.* }

INGREDIENTS

1 cup (250 mL) butter
3/4 cup (175 mL) granulated sugar
1/4 cup (60 mL) brown sugar, packed
1 egg, lightly beaten
1 tsp (5 mL) vanilla extract
2 cups (500 mL) all-purpose flour
1 tsp (5 mL) cream of tartar
1/4 tsp (1 mL) salt
1 tsp (5 mL) baking soda
3/4 tsp (4 mL) ground nutmeg

METHOD

Preheat oven to 350°F (180°C). Line two baking sheets with parchment paper and set aside.

In a bowl, cream together the butter with the granulated sugar and brown sugar. Add the egg and blend well, then stir in the vanilla.

In another bowl, sift together the flour, cream of tartar, salt, baking soda and nutmeg, and then stir into the creamed mixture.

Turn the dough out onto a floured surface, then roll out to a thickness of 1/2 in (12 mm). Cut into rounds using 2-in (5-cm) cookie cutter and place on the baking sheet.

Bake for 8 to 10 minutes.

Yield: 3 dozen cookies

BEST SCOTTISH
SHORTBREAD

{ *The earliest known references to shortbread date back to the twelfth century, but initially it was simply bread dough that was left to dry. What we know now as shortbread, the deliciously simple cookie, became popular in the sixteenth century. Other fats have been popular in baking, such as lard or vegetable shortening, but the key to shortbread is butter. I love shortbread right after it comes out of the oven of course, but even more so after it is stored for a while, as it obtains a full nutty flavour. But you'll have to hide it for that to happen!* }

INGREDIENTS

1 cup (250 mL) butter
½ cup (125 mL) icing sugar
2 cups (500 mL) all-purpose flour, sifted

METHOD

Preheat oven to 375°F (190°C). Line a baking sheet with parchment paper and set aside.

In a bowl, cream the butter until soft, and beat in the sugar gradually. Stir flour in well.

Turn the dough out onto the centre of the baking sheet and pat it into a circle about ¾-in (20-mm) thick and 7 in (18 cm) in diameter. Crimp the outer edge of the dough between your fingers, and prick it all over with the tines of a fork. Cover loosely with plastic wrap and chill for at least a half hour, until quite firm.

Remove the plastic wrap and bake for 5 minutes, then reduce heat to 300°F (150°C) and bake for about 45 minutes longer. The shortbread should be pale gold, not brown, when done.

While still warm, cut into 16 small wedges. This is rich, and disappears fast.

Yield: 16 cookies

BUTTERY
SHORTBREAD COOKIES

{ *This is a popular type of shortbread cookie, formed into individual cookies rather than a cake cut into wedges as in the recipe for Best Scottish Shortbread (page 18). It makes wonderful Christmas cookies, easily cut out into custom shapes for decorating with icing and sprinkles. Homemade shortbread is quite simple to make, and far superior in texture and flavour than store-bought! Some of my fondest memories include exceedingly messy afternoons of Christmas cookie decorating with my kids.* }

INGREDIENTS

1 cup (250 mL) butter
½ cup (125 mL) icing sugar
¾ cup (175 mL) cornstarch
1 ¼ cups (300 mL) all-purpose flour

METHOD

Preheat oven to 300°F (150°C). Line two baking sheets with parchment paper and set aside.

In a bowl, cream the butter until it is soft and fluffy. Add in the sugar, cornstarch and then flour gradually, mixing and kneading with fingers until it is well blended.

Turn the dough out onto a floured surface, then roll it out to a thickness of ⅓ in (8 mm). Cut out the dough with seasonal or 2-in (5-cm) cookie cutters.

Bake for 30 minutes, or until lightly golden.

Yield: 2 dozen cookies

INGONISH
OATCAKES

{ *Historically, oats were grown in Cape Breton, having come from Scotland with settlers, who had it as a staple food. Lard was the predominant fat used for baking and cooking for many years, rendered from pigs that were used to clear land and provide food for families. It can be found at your local grocery store, and is the key to the success of this recipe. It really helps these oatcakes obtain a delicious crispiness.* }

INGREDIENTS

3 cups (750 mL) rolled oats, plus extra for rolling
3 cups (750 mL) all-purpose flour
1 cup (250 mL) granulated sugar
2 tsp (10 mL) salt
1 tsp (5 mL) baking soda
1 1/2 cups (375 mL) lard, vegetable shortening or a mix of butter and shortening, cubed
3/4 cup (175 mL) cold water

METHOD

Preheat oven to 350°F (180°C). Line baking sheets with parchment paper and set aside.

In a bowl, whisk together the rolled oats, flour, sugar, salt and baking soda. Using fingertips or pastry cutters, blend in the lard or butter and shortening into the dry mixture, until the largest pieces are the same size as small peas.

Stir in just enough cold water to make a dough.

Turn the dough out onto a surface covered with extra rolled oats, and then roll it out to a thickness of 1/4 in (5 mm).

Cut into squares, place on the baking sheet and bake for about 15 minutes, until lightly golden.

Yield: 5 dozen oatcakes

LEMON RAISIN
COOKIE SANDWICH

Raisins, always the most available dried fruit, make a delicious filling for a sandwich-style cookie. You'll need to have prepared 1 batch of dough for Old-Fashioned Sugar Cookies (page 16).

INGREDIENTS

Raisin Filling

1 cup (250 mL) raisins
½ cup (125 mL) water
½ cup (125 mL) granulated sugar
1 tbsp (15 mL) all-purpose flour
1 tbsp (15 mL) lemon juice
1 tsp (5 mL) lemon zest

Cookies

Dough for 1 batch Old-Fashioned Sugar Cookies (page 16)

METHOD

In a large pot on medium heat, cook together the raisins, water and sugar. Whisk in the flour and lower the heat, stirring occasionally. Cook slowly until thick, approximately 10 minutes.

Stir in the lemon juice and lemon zest, and let cool.

Preheat oven to 350°F (180°C). Line a baking sheet with parchment paper and set aside.

Cut out rolled sugar cookie dough with a 3-in (8-cm) or larger round cookie cutter. Put a teaspoon of Raisin Filling on each round of dough. Cover with another round and press the edges together to seal, then prick with a fork.

Bake for 10 to 12 minutes, until golden.

Yield: 18 cookies

OAT
CRACKERS

This recipe came to Nova Scotia hundreds of years ago with the early settlers from the Highlands of Scotland. It was served at an afternoon tea to Princess Elizabeth on the occasion of her visit to Halifax in November 1951. It is unsweetened, with the flavour of the oats themselves providing a gentle sweetness. These are more like crackers than cookies, and are excellent with savoury toppings, like cheeses or jellies, or simply spread with butter. There is no flour in these crackers, which may appeal to those trying to avoid gluten (make sure that the oats you get are marked "gluten free" to avoid cross-contamination).

INGREDIENTS

4 cups (1 L) ground oats (process rolled oats to a fine texture in a food processor)
3/4 tsp (4 mL) baking soda
Pinch of salt
2 tbsp (30 mL) vegetable shortening
2 tbsp (30 mL) butter
3/4 cup (175 mL) milk, or as much as needed

METHOD

Preheat oven to 400°F (200°C). Line a baking sheet with parchment paper and set aside.

In a bowl, whisk together the ground oats with the baking soda and salt. Using your fingertips or pastry cutters, blend in the shortening and butter until the largest pieces are the same size as small peas. Slowly mix in enough milk to make a fairly soft dough.

Turn the dough out onto a floured surface and then roll it out to a thickness of 1/8 in (3 mm). Cut in squares or strips. Place onto the baking sheet and bake until lightly golden, around 8 minutes.

Yield: 4 dozen crackers

OATBREAD
CRISPS

Oatbread is another term for oatcakes, which is a more commonly used term now, but it is a good way to differentiate this savoury version from the sweet kind. The lack of sugar (which suggests that this is an older recipe) makes this crisp. It is natural to think only of the ocean when thinking of Nova Scotia, but there are so many rivers that grist and other sorts of mills sprang up everywhere, including Cape Breton, where locally grown oats were milled. These are really tasty with a bowl of stew or soup, and some thin slices of sharp cheese.

INGREDIENTS

2 cups (500 mL) fine ground oats (process rolled oats in a food processor until fine), plus extra for rolling
1 ½ cups (375 mL) all-purpose flour
½ tsp (2.5 mL) baking soda
2 tsp (10 mL) baking powder
½ tsp (2.5 mL) salt
½ cup (125 mL) shortening or lard (less 1 tbsp)
½ cup (125 mL) cold water

METHOD

Preheat oven to 350°F (180°C). Line baking sheets with parchment paper and set aside.

In a bowl, whisk together the ground oats, flour, baking soda, baking powder and salt. Using pastry cutters or your fingertips, blend in the shortening until the largest pieces are the same size as small peas. Mix in the cold water.

Turn the dough out onto a surface covered with extra ground rolled oats, and then roll it out to a thickness of ¼ in (5 mm). Cut the dough into squares.

Place on the baking sheet and bake for around 10 minutes, until lightly browned.

Yield: 3 dozen biscuits

Cakes

NEIGHBOURLY
POUND CAKE

Pound cakes traditionally were composed of a pound each of flour, sugar, butter and eggs, and were meant to be showcase cakes featuring expensive ingredients. Early recipes date back to the 1700s and were often made by two people. Neighbours would help each other – one to beat the mixture by hand and the other to sift the flour and beat the eggs. The more it's beaten, the finer the texture, and the lighter the cake. There's a lot of stirring to this cake. It's fun to do it the old-fashioned way, but you could cheat and use a food mixer. Either way, you'll end up with a rich, buttery, tender cake. Pound cakes take a long time to cook, so be patient.

INGREDIENTS

2 cups (475 mL) butter, room temperature
4 cups (1 L) granulated sugar
8 large eggs, separated (or 9 medium or 10 small)
4 cups (1 L) all-purpose flour, well sifted
1/4 tsp (1 mL) salt
1 tsp (5 mL) lemon extract

METHOD

Preheat oven to 300°F (150°C). Grease a loaf pan, line the bottom with parchment paper and set aside.

In a bowl, cream together the butter and sugar until light and fluffy.

In a separate bowl, beat the egg yolks well, then add these gradually to the butter and sugar mixture, beating well after each addition.

In a large bowl, beat the egg whites with a handheld electric mixer on medium until they form stiff peaks.

In another bowl, sift the flour and salt together.

Fold the egg whites in small amounts into the butter and egg yolk mixture, alternating with small amounts of the flour mixture, and beat well after each addition. Add the lemon extract and blend well.

Pour into the pan, and bake for 3 hours, until a cake tester comes out clean, with just a few crumbs.

Yield: 10 to 12 servings

NEVER FAIL
POUND CAKE

This is a lighter variation of the Neighbourly Pound Cake (page 26), with more ingredients but less weight of each. The addition of baking powder, which was first introduced to home baking in the early 1900s, eliminates the necessity of a lot of sifting of the flour – which was the earlier way of incorporating air and loft into a batter. This recipe makes a delicious base for a delightful white fruit cake: just add in the optional candied cherries, raisins and candied pineapple. I like this on a plate with the traditional Dundee Fruit Cake (page 34) at Christmas time.

INGREDIENTS

1 cup (250 mL) granulated sugar
1 cup (250 mL) butter
3 eggs, separated
2 cups (500 mL) all-purpose flour, sifted
1 tsp (5 mL) baking powder
½ cup (125 mL) milk
1 tsp (5 mL) vanilla extract
1 tsp (5 mL) lemon extract
⅓ cup (75 mL) each of candied cherries, raisins and candied
  pineapple, diced (optional)

METHOD

Preheat oven to 350°F (180°C). Grease a loaf pan, line the bottom with parchment paper and set aside.

In a large bowl, cream the sugar and butter together vigorously until softened. Add the egg yolks and beat thoroughly.

In another bowl, sift together the flour with the baking powder.

Add the flour mixture, alternating with the milk, to the egg yolk mixture and mix gently. If you wish to make this into a white fruit cake, add in the diced candied cherries, raisins and candied pineapple at this point. Mix in the vanilla and lemon extracts.

Beat the egg whites with a handheld electric mixer until they form soft peaks, then gently fold them into the batter.

Turn the mixture into the loaf pan and bake for 1 to 1 ½ hours, until a cake tester comes out clean.

Yield: 10 to 12 servings

BEST BERRY
MUFFINS

This sort of muffin, a sweet quick bread, would have been a later addition to Nova Scotian diets. Muffins used to mean "English muffins," an entirely different sort of quick bread. The invention and introduction of baking powder to the household kitchen revolutionized baking, allowing for the quick preparation of unyeasted but lofty cakes and breads. Add any fresh local berries to the batter to add that pop of juicy flavour! So wonderful warm out of the oven for breakfast or a mid-morning snack.

INGREDIENTS

¼ cup (60 mL) butter, softened
⅓ cup (75 mL) granulated sugar
1 egg, beaten
2 ⅓ cups (575 mL) all-purpose flour (first amount)
1 tbsp + 1 tsp (20 mL) baking powder
½ tsp (2.5 mL) salt
⅓ cup (75 mL) all-purpose flour (second amount)
1 cup (250 mL) fresh blueberries, raspberries, strawberries,
   blackberries or a mix
1 cup (250 mL) milk

METHOD

Preheat oven to 400°F (200°C). Grease a 12-cup muffin tin and set aside.

In a bowl, cream the butter until it's soft, then gradually add the sugar and egg.

In a smaller bowl, sift together the first amount of flour, baking powder and salt.

In another bowl, toss the second amount of flour with the berries, then add them to the butter mixture, alternating with the milk.

Distribute the batter in the muffin tin. Bake for about 25 to 30 minutes.

Yield: 12 muffins

CLASSIC
SPONGE CAKE

Sponge cakes have a long history — with the earliest recipes recorded back in the 1600s in Europe — and this recipe was no doubt brought to Nova Scotia with the earliest European settlers. This is a classic sponge cake — an exceptionally light and springy cake, with eggs providing the moisture and height, instead of butter and baking powder. As with the pound cake recipes, the original instructions call for two people to make this cake, but electricity has helped to streamline the process. It is excellent on its own or with a scattering of fresh berries on top, especially in the summer, when a light dessert is even more appealing.

INGREDIENTS

10 eggs, separated
4 cups (1 L) granulated sugar
2 cups (500 mL) cake and pastry flour
2 tbsp (30 mL) lemon juice
Grated rind of 1 lemon
Dusting of icing sugar to serve

METHOD

Preheat oven to 350°F (180°C). Line a 16-cup (4-L) tube pan or bundt pan with parchment paper (do not grease) and set aside.

In a large bowl, whisk the egg yolks until light and lemon-coloured. Gradually stir the sugar into the egg yolks. Gently fold the flour in to the egg yolk mixture. Add the lemon juice and rind.

In a separate large bowl, beat the egg whites with a handheld electric mixer until they form stiff peaks. Fold the egg whites into the yolk mixture.

Pour the mixture into the pan and bake for 30 to 45 minutes, until golden brown and the top springs back when pressed firmly.

Invert the pan over a sturdy bottle or kitchen funnel and let the cake cool completely upside down for 2 to 3 hours before releasing from the pan. Dust with icing sugar before serving.

Yield: 12 servings

CENTENNIAL
LEMON CAKE

This recipe was more than a hundred years old when Canada was a mere baby! This is a quasi-pound cake — lots of butter, sugar and eggs, with the lovely scent and flavour of fresh lemon. A good "keeping cake," although it might not last all that long, tasting this good!

INGREDIENTS

1 cup (250 mL) butter
3 cups (750 mL) icing sugar
5 eggs
4 cups (1 L) cake and pastry flour
1 tsp (5 mL) baking powder
1 cup (250 mL) of light cream or milk
1 lemon, zested and juiced

METHOD

Preheat oven to 300°F (150°C). Grease a 9-in by 9-in (23-cm by 23-cm) square pan, and set aside.

In a bowl, cream together the butter and sugar until light and fluffy. Add the eggs individually to the butter and sugar mixture, beating well after each addition.

In another bowl, sift together the flour with the baking powder. Add the flour mixture to the creamed butter and sugar mixture. Add the cream or milk and rind and juice of lemon, and mix gently.

Pour into the prepared pan and bake for 2 to 2 ½ hours, until a cake tester comes out clean, with a few crumbs.

Yield: 12 servings

AUNT MARY'S
DARK FRUIT CAKE

"Aunt Mary" is a legendary character who made the dark fruit cake — also known as a "wedding cake" — that would be put under the pillows of young women to conjure up their future husband. Aunt Mary was very proprietary about this and would never give you the method. But I will! This recipe can be divided in half if you don't want to give it out to your entire neighbourhood. The addition of red wine was a new element to me, and it adds a layer of depth to the already complex spiciness of the cake. This cake only gets better with time.

INGREDIENTS

7 cups (1 kg) raisins
7 cups (1 kg) currants
5 cups (1.25 L) all-purpose flour
1 tsp (5 mL) baking powder
2 cups (475 mL) butter, room temperature
2 ¼ cups (535 mL) granulated sugar
10 eggs, lightly beaten
¾ cup (175 mL) brandy
¾ cup (175 mL) red wine
1 tbsp (15 mL) ground cloves
1 tbsp (15 mL) ground allspice
2 tbsp (30 mL) ground cinnamon
1 tsp (5 mL) ground nutmeg
1 tsp (5 mL) blanched sliced almonds
⅓ cup (80 mL) candied lemon peel, diced
¾ cup (175 mL) molasses

METHOD

Preheat oven to 300°F (150°C). Grease two 9-in (22-cm) tube pans, line the bottoms with parchment paper and set aside.

In a large paper bag or large bowl, toss the raisins and currants with 2 cups (500 mL) of the flour, or however much is needed to coat them evenly, then mix in the baking powder.

In another very large bowl, cream together the butter and sugar until fluffy. Stir in the eggs, beating until combined thoroughly. Stir in the brandy and red wine, the spices, the almonds, lemon peel and molasses.

Once all the liquid ingredients are well combined, stir in the dried fruit. Gradually stir in the remaining flour. This may test your arm, as the mixture will get quite stiff by the end — have friends and family take turns stirring.

Pour the batter into the prepared pans and bake for 3 hours, or until a cake tester comes out clean.

Yield: 24 servings

DUNDEE
FRUIT CAKE

This is a classic recipe for the most iconic fruit cake, originating in Dundee, Scotland, and initially made popular in Nova Scotia by early Scottish settlers. It's popular for a reason — the proportions of the ingredients are ideal for a dense, nuanced, aromatic cake — and the flavour of the almonds is a lovely note throughout. This is a workout cake — we can call it resistance stirring — as you mix together the dry and wet ingredients.

INGREDIENTS

1 cup (250 mL) butter
1 cup (250 mL) sugar
5 eggs
½ cup (125 mL) ground almonds
2 ¼ cups (550 mL) all-purpose flour
1 tsp (5 mL) baking powder
¼ tsp (1 mL) salt
1 cup (250 mL) golden or sultana raisins
1 cup (250 mL) currants
¼ cup (60 mL) mixed candied fruit, chopped
1 tbsp (15 mL) grated orange rind
2 tbsp (30 mL) orange juice
Almond halves, strips of citron and/or candied cherries, to
   decorate

METHOD

Preheat oven to 300°F (150°C). Grease a bundt pan or a 9-in (22-cm) tube pan, line the bottom with parchment paper and set aside.

In a large bowl, cream the butter and sugar together. Beat in the eggs, one at a time, then mix in the ground almonds.

In another bowl, sift together the flour, baking powder and salt. Mix in the raisins, currants and candied fruit. Add this dry mixture to the wet mixture, stirring it in well, then add the grated orange rind and juice.

Pour the batter into the prepared pan, pressing down with the flat of a spoon to eliminate any air bubbles. Decorate the top with almond halves and strips of citron and candied cherries.

Bake for about 1 hour and 15 minutes, or until a cake tester comes out clean.

Yield: 10 to 12 servings

WAR CAKE

> *War cake recipes were popular starting in World War I, with rations and scarcity dictating the minimal use of sugar, butter, eggs, nuts and dried fruits. Raisins were the most readily available dried fruit during both World Wars, as well as the Depression, and they are a good sweetener. They also help keep the cake moist and last longer. The add-ins are optional, but add more texture and flavour. This can also serve as a quick Christmas cake, as well as a lovely cake to share with visitors.*

INGREDIENTS

2 cups (500 mL) seedless raisins (or other fruit)
1 cup (250 mL) water
1 cup (250 mL) brown sugar, packed
½ cup (125 mL) butter
½ tsp (2.5 mL) salt
½ tsp (2.5 mL) ground cinnamon
½ tsp (2.5 mL) ground nutmeg
½ tsp (2.5 mL) ground cloves
2 cups (500 mL) all-purpose flour
1 tsp (5 mL) baking soda
1 tsp (5 mL) vanilla extract

Optional
2 cups (500 mL) mixed chopped peel, nuts, figs and prunes
   (combined with or in place of the raisins for a total of 2 cups
   [500 mL])

METHOD

Preheat oven to 325°F (170°C). Grease a loaf pan, line the bottom with parchment paper and set aside.

Place the raisins, water, brown sugar, butter, salt, cinnamon, nutmeg and cloves into a large pot and bring to a boil. Lower the heat and let simmer for 6 minutes. Set the mixture aside to cool until it is room temperature.

In a medium bowl, sift together the flour and baking soda, then add to the cooled mixture. Stir well, and add the vanilla extract.

If using the optional dried fruits and nuts, add them in at this point.

Turn the dough into the pan and bake for 1 ½ to 2 hours, until a cake tester comes out clean, with a few crumbs.

Yield: 12 servings

CINNAMON APPLE
GINGERBREAD

The spices of gingerbread with the addition of apples scent the air with warmth. The smells evoke memories of wood smoke, the feel of chillier mornings and morning fog lingering on the lake. A perfect Nova Scotia autumnal or winter dessert. This cake comes together very quickly and keeps well, too. The addition of the sauce with the apples adds a textural richness — I love the depth and satisfying heaviness of this authentic gingerbread.

INGREDIENTS

½ cup (125 mL) water
½ cup (125 mL) granulated sugar (first amount)
3 apples, peeled, cored and quartered
¼ cup (60 mL) butter
⅓ cup (75 mL) granulated sugar (second amount)
1 egg, lightly beaten
⅓ cup (75 mL) molasses
1 cup (250 mL) all-purpose flour
½ tsp (2.5 mL) baking soda
½ tsp (2.5 mL) salt
1 tsp (5 mL) ground ginger
1 tsp (5 mL) ground cinnamon
¼ tsp (1 mL) ground cloves
⅓ cup (75 mL) buttermilk

METHOD

Preheat oven to 325°F (170°C). Butter a 10-in by 6 ½-in (25-cm by 17-cm) baking dish and set aside.

In a large pot, bring the water to a boil over high heat, and then add the first amount of sugar. Boil for 3 minutes.

Reduce the heat to medium, add the apples and cook until almost tender, around 5 minutes. Pour the apples and syrup into the baking dish and let cool.

In a bowl, cream the butter and second amount of sugar together well, until soft and fluffy. Add the egg and molasses and beat well.

In another bowl, whisk together the flour, baking soda, salt and spices. Gently stir the dry mixture into the butter and sugar mixture, alternating with the buttermilk, stirring as little as possible to make a smooth batter.

Pour the batter over the cooked apples in the pan. Bake for 50 minutes, or until a cake tester comes out clean.

Tastes good served with Brown Sugar Sauce (page 123).

Yield: 12 servings

BOILED RAISIN
SPICE CAKE

{ *Raisins show up in a lot of older cake recipes as an affordable sweetener that also provides moistness and depth. It is an extremely straightforward name, as was the style in older recipes. It's truthful: this does in fact involve a quantity of boiled raisins! It's a good keeping cake to have on hand, and the smell of the rich spices really warms up your home as it bakes.* }

INGREDIENTS

2 cups (500 mL) raisins
3 cups (750 mL) water
½ cup (125 mL) butter
1 cup (250 mL) brown sugar
1 egg, lightly beaten
2 cups (500 mL) all-purpose flour
1 tsp (5 mL) baking powder
½ tsp (2.5 mL) baking soda
½ tsp (2.5 mL) ground cinnamon
½ tsp (2.5 mL) ground nutmeg
¼ tsp (1 mL) ground allspice
¼ tsp (1 mL) salt
1 tsp (5 mL) vanilla extract

METHOD

Preheat oven to 350°F (180°C). Grease a loaf pan, line the bottom with parchment paper and set aside.

In a large pot, mix the raisins with the water and boil on high heat until thick, and approximately 1 cup (250 mL) water is left. Remove the pot from the heat, and while the mixture is still hot, add butter and brown sugar. Mix in and let the mixture cool to room temperature. Whisk in the egg.

In a bowl, sift together the flour with baking powder, baking soda, the spices and salt. Stir the dry ingredients into the wet mixture, then add the vanilla extract.

Pour into the prepared pan, then bake for 45 minutes, or until a cake tester comes out clean, with a few crumbs.

Yield: 12 servings

HOT COFFEE
FRUIT LOAF

This fruit cake was initially made with pork fat, cut from the pig during the butchering process, then put through a meat grinder – not so strange when you think of the traditional recipes for mincemeat. Although lard is still a primary ingredient, it doesn't dominate the flavour of the cake. The fat melts into the cake during the baking process and makes for a rich, moist cake. If you're not sure about this one, I recommend dividing the recipe in half – this makes two substantial loaves!

INGREDIENTS

2 cups (470 mL) lard
2 cups (500 mL) strong freshly brewed hot coffee
1 cup (250 mL) brown sugar, packed
1 cup (250 mL) molasses
2 eggs
5 cups (1.25 L) all-purpose flour (first amount)
1 tsp (5 mL) baking soda
1 tsp (5 mL) ground cloves
1 tsp (5 mL) cinnamon
2 $\frac{3}{4}$ cups (670 mL) raisins
2 $\frac{3}{4}$ cups (670 mL) dates, chopped
3 cups (750 mL) mixed peel, diced
1 $\frac{2}{3}$ cups (400 mL) almonds, chopped
$\frac{3}{4}$ cup (180 mL) dried figs, chopped (optional)
$\frac{1}{2}$ cup (125 mL) all-purpose flour (second amount)

METHOD

Preheat oven to 300°F (150°C). Grease two 9-in (22-cm) tube pans, line the bottoms with parchment paper and set aside.

In a large pot on medium heat, melt the lard, and then stir in the hot coffee. Set aside the pot and let cool to room temperature. Transfer the cooled coffee mixture to a large bowl. Whisk in the brown sugar, molasses and eggs, stirring well.

In another large bowl, sift first amount of flour together with the baking soda, cloves and cinnamon. Stir the dry mixture into the coffee mixture well.

In a medium bowl, stir together the fruit and nuts with the second amount of flour. Combine well with the batter.

Fill the two pans with the batter, then bake for around 2 hours, until a cake tester comes out clean.

Yield: 24 servings

MAPLE WALNUT
CAKE

{ *Nova Scotia has a lot of maple syrup producers for its size — around 150 farms that produce 57,000 gallons of syrup per year. A day spent at a maple farm tasting fresh syrup is a highlight of the winter for many families. This delicious cake is imbued with the flavour of maple, but if you want a stronger maple taste, use a mix of maple and granulated sugar instead of just granulated sugar. I prefer the flavour and texture of toasted nuts — toast them in the preheated oven for 8 to 10 minutes if this is your preference, too.* }

INGREDIENTS

½ cup (125 mL) butter
½ cup (125 mL) granulated sugar (or ¼ cup [60 mL] granulated sugar plus ¼ cup [60 mL] maple sugar)
½ cup (125 mL) maple syrup
1 tsp (5 mL) vanilla extract
2 eggs, beaten
1 ¾ cup (425 mL) all-purpose flour
2 ½ tsp (12 mL) baking powder
½ tsp (2.5 mL) salt
¼ cup (60 mL) milk
½ cup (125 mL) chopped walnuts, toasted if desired

METHOD

Preheat oven to 350°F (180°C). Grease an 8-in by 8-in (25-cm by 25-cm) square pan and set aside.

In a bowl, cream together the butter and sugar until light and fluffy. Add maple syrup a little at a time, mixing well, then stir in vanilla extract. Stir in the eggs.

In a separate bowl, sift together the flour, baking powder and salt. Add the dry ingredients to the wet ingredients, alternating with milk. Stir in the nuts.

Pour the batter into the pan and bake for 30 minutes or until a cake tester comes out clean, with crumbs.

Yield: 12 servings

LEMON BLUEBERRY
CAKE

This is a classic summertime quick cake, and should be eaten quickly – not a hard task with delicious fresh blueberries! Have it with a scoop of Homemade Vanilla Ice Cream (page 111), which is an appealing contrast to the still-warm cake. One of the lovely things about blueberries in Nova Scotia is that there are often two crops over the mid and late summer, and there are plenty of options for getting your fill. You can scoop them off the wild low bushes on your walks through the woods, or go on berry-picking jaunts to your local blueberry farm. They freeze well, so they can be used in baked goods year-round.

INGREDIENTS

½ cup (125 mL) butter

1 cup (250 mL) sugar

2 eggs, beaten

2 cups (500 mL) all-purpose flour, sifted

2 tsp (10 mL) baking powder

¾ cup (175 mL) milk

Zest of 1 lemon

1 cup (250 mL) blueberries, tossed with 2 tbsp (30 mL) all-purpose flour

¾ cup (175 mL) packed brown sugar

¼ tsp (1 mL) ground cinnamon

METHOD

Preheat oven to 350°F (180°C). Grease a 9-in by 9-in (23-cm by 23-cm) square pan, and set aside.

In a bowl, cream together the butter and sugar until light and fluffy. Add beaten eggs, and mix well.

In a separate bowl, sift together the flour and baking powder. Stir into the wet ingredients, alternating with the milk. Stir in the lemon zest, and gently fold in the floured blueberries.

Pour batter into prepared pan. In a small bowl, mix brown sugar and cinnamon together. Sprinkle on top of batter and bake for 35 to 40 minutes, or until a cake tester comes out clean, with crumbs.

Yield: 12 servings

SPICED CRUMB
CAKE

I love the simplicity of the names of many of these recipes. Yes, it is a crumb cake, and in this case the crumbs are inside the cake and on top of it as well, like a streusel. It makes a lovely breakfast cake and it's also perfect for social gatherings, with coffee or tea. It's a satisfying mix of textures and gently spiced sweetness. This fills the platonic ideal of a coffee cake!

INGREDIENTS

2 cups (500 mL) all-purpose flour
1 cup (250 mL) granulated sugar
Pinch of salt
1 tsp (5 mL) ground allspice
1 tsp (5 mL) ground cinnamon
1 tsp (5 mL) ground cloves
3/4 cup (175 mL) cold butter, cubed
1 tsp (5 mL) baking soda
1 cup (250 mL) buttermilk
1 egg, lightly beaten
1 cup (250 mL), or more, raisins

METHOD

Preheat oven to 350°F (180°C). Grease an 8-in (25-cm) pie plate and set aside.

In a bowl, whisk together the flour, sugar, salt and spices. Using a pastry cutter or fingertips, work the cold butter into the dry mixture until it resembles large peas. Remove 1 cup (250 mL) of mixture and set aside.

In a separate bowl, stir the baking soda into the buttermilk, then add the egg, the bowl of crumb mixture and raisins.

Turn the batter into the pie plate. Sprinkle with the cup of dry mixture. Bake for around 45 minutes, until nicely browned and a cake tester comes out clean, with crumbs.

Yield: 8 servings

CLASSIC
DOUGHNUTS

{ *There are more doughnut shops per capita in Canada than anywhere else on the planet. Originally brought to North America by Dutch immigrants, doughnuts caught on in a big way by the mid-1800s, and that included Nova Scotia. These old-fashioned doughnuts were often called "fried cakes." The yeast gives them a nice airy loft, quite irresistible, and a classic version to have with a hot cup of coffee.* }

INGREDIENTS

2 cups (500 mL) vegetable oil, for frying
2 ¼ tsp (11 mL) or 1 packet dry yeast
1 cup (250 mL) milk, heated to 110°F (45°C)
1 cup (250 mL) all-purpose flour (first amount)
2 eggs, lightly beaten
½ cup (125 mL) granulated sugar
¼ cup (60 mL) butter, melted
½ tsp (2.5 mL) salt
½ tsp (2.5 mL) ground mace
4 cups (1 L) all-purpose flour (second amount)
2 cups (500 mL) icing sugar, for dusting

METHOD

Fill a heavy-bottomed pot with the vegetable oil and set aside on the stovetop. Line two baking sheets with parchment paper and set aside.

In a large bowl, dissolve the yeast in the milk and whisk in the first amount of flour. Cover with plastic wrap, and allow to rise until double in bulk, around 30 minutes.

Add the eggs, sugar, melted butter, salt and mace. Beat this mixture thoroughly and add the second amount of flour, making into a dough.

Turn out onto a floured surface, and knead the dough until it is smooth and elastic. It should be moist but not sticky. Cover the dough with a damp towel and let it double in bulk, around 30 minutes to 1 hour.

Gently push down the dough to remove any bubbles, then roll it out to a thickness of ¾ in (20 mm). With a sharp knife, cut the dough into long strips about ¾-in (20-mm) wide. Take each strip and shape it into a figure eight. Alternatively you may use doughnut or cookie cutters to cut the dough into 3-in (6-cm) rounds with 1-in (2-cm) holes.

Arrange the doughnuts on the prepared baking sheets, leaving at least 1 in (2 cm) between doughnuts. Cover the doughnuts loosely with plastic wrap and let them proof in a warm place until almost doubled in size, 30 to 40 minutes.

Check to see if the doughnuts are ready every 5 to 10 minutes. To test, use a fingertip to lightly touch one of the doughnuts. If the dough springs back immediately, it needs more time; if it springs back slowly, it's ready; and if the dough doesn't spring back at all, it's over-proofed. You can punch down and reroll over-proofed dough once.

Heat the oil until it registers 350°F (180°C) on a deep-fry thermometer. Working in batches, use a slotted metal spoon or spatula to carefully place the doughnuts in the hot oil. Fry, flipping once, until light golden brown, 1 to 2 minutes per side. Transfer as done to a wire rack and return the oil to 350°F (180°C) between batches. Let the doughnuts cool, then dust with icing sugar if desired before serving.

Yield: 3 dozen doughnuts

SCOTTISH
SCONES

{ *In Scotland, the terms "bannock" and "scone" are often used interchangeably, but traditionally bannock is a rather large, round cake, and the scone is a smaller triangle cut from the round of dough before baking. In Nova Scotia we usually use the term "scone." This is probably one of the older quick breads out there, and it makes for a quick, satisfying and filling meal, especially paired with tea or coffee and some accompaniments like butter, jam and cheese.* }

INGREDIENTS

2 cups (500 mL) all-purpose flour
2 tsp (10 mL) baking powder
1/2 tsp (2.5 mL) salt
2 tsp (10 mL) granulated sugar
4 tbsp (60 mL) cold butter, cubed
1 egg, beaten
1/2 cup (125 mL) half-and-half cream (10% mf)

METHOD

Preheat oven to 450°F (230°C). Line a baking sheet with parchment paper and set aside.

In a bowl, sift together the flour, baking powder, salt and sugar. Using two knives or a pastry cutter, cut in the butter, then add the egg and cream. Blend just enough to mix.

Turn out onto a floured surface. Knead lightly. Roll out to a thickness of 1/2 in (5 mm). Cut into triangles, place on the baking sheet and bake for 15 minutes.

Serve hot with lots of butter and jam.

Yield: 8 scones

GOVERNMENT HOUSE
TEA BISCUITS

The following recipe was prepared and served at Government House for the visit of King George VI and Queen Elizabeth, on June 15, 1939. These are a delicate, thin scone — essentially a tea biscuit. They are easy to re-split and fill with a wedge of sharp cheddar or another side.

INGREDIENTS

3 cups (750 mL) all-purpose flour
¼ cup (60 mL) granulated sugar
2 tsp (10 mL) baking powder
3 tbsp (45 mL) cold butter, cubed
1 egg, beaten
1 cup (250 mL) milk

METHOD

Preheat oven to 350°F (180°C). Line a baking sheet with parchment paper and set aside.

In a bowl sift together the flour, sugar and baking powder. Using two knives or a pastry cutter, cut in the butter, then add the egg and milk. Blend just enough to mix.

Turn out onto a floured surface. Roll out to a thickness of ¼ in (5 mm). Cut into rounds using 2-in (5-cm) cutter.

Place on baking sheet and bake for 20 minutes.

Yield: 12 biscuits

LUNENBURG
SKILLET SCONES

{ *Originally bannock was cooked on a griddle on top of a fire, and this recipe harkens back to this form. This recipe came with Scottish immigrants who settled in Lunenburg on the South Shore of Nova Scotia. I like the flavour that the skillet imparts. These really are best eaten straight out of the pan, with a melting pat of butter.* }

INGREDIENTS

1 cup (250 mL) all-purpose flour
2 tsp (10 mL) baking powder
Pinch of salt
1/3 cup (75 mL) milk

METHOD

In a bowl, sift together the flour, baking powder and salt. Mix in the milk until you have a slightly damp, sticky dough.

Divide the dough into 6 round cakes and cook on a lightly greased skillet over medium heat. Flip the scones over after around 4 minutes and cook for a few more minutes until golden. Eat while nice and warm!

Yield: 6 scones

Pies

PERFECT
PASTRY

This is a recipe for a classic lard-based pastry, which is the traditional pastry, pre-dating (of course!) vegetable shortening, and a very different flavour from an all-butter pastry. All are good, of course, but very different experiences. Please don't shy away from this — it is really excellent — and if you have an opportunity to buy the lard from a local farmer, even better (although you can also find it at your grocery store). This is closest to the flavour of pies that were eaten over the past couple of hundred years. It makes for a tender and flaky crust.

INGREDIENTS

2 cups (500 mL) all-purpose flour, sifted
1 tsp (5 mL) salt
2/3 cup (150 mL) cold lard, diced
1/4 cup (60 mL) ice water

METHOD

In a large bowl, whisk together the flour and salt. Using a pastry cutter, or two knives, cut in 1/3 cup (75 mL) lard into the flour mixture until it resembles cornmeal. Cut in the other 1/3 cup (75 mL) of lard much more coarsely — so that the mixture ends up looking like it has fat the size of peas.

Sprinkle the cold water 1 tbsp (15 mL) at a time over the mixture and mix together lightly with a fork until the flour is moistened. Press firmly into a ball, and cut in half.

These may be rolled out, or wrapped in waxed paper in refrigerator until needed.

Yield: Pastry for 9-in (23-cm) double crust pie

TENDER
PASTRY

{ *This makes for an exceptionally tender and flaky crust, with a wonderful flavour. The Perfect Pastry (page 52) is very good too, but not quite as tender. They are two very different types of pie crusts, both equally good but with notably individual qualities. Double this to make sure you have extra dough in your freezer should a pie-making mood descend!* }

INGREDIENTS

2 ½ cups (625 mL) all-purpose flour
1 tsp (5 mL) salt
2 tbsp (30 mL) granulated sugar
13 tbsp (195 mL) cold butter, cubed
8 tbsp (120 mL) cold lard, cubed
4 tbsp (60 mL) to 6 tbsp (90 mL) ice water

METHOD

In a large bowl, whisk together the flour, salt and sugar. Using a pastry cutter, or two knives, cut the butter into the flour mixture until the mixture resembles cornmeal. Then cut in the lard much more coarsely, so that the mixture ends up looking like it has fat the size of peas.

Sprinkle the cold water 1 tbsp (15 mL) at a time over the mixture to dampen it in several places and then mix together lightly with a fork until the flour is moistened. Press firmly into a ball, and cut in half.

These may be rolled out, or wrapped in waxed paper and stored in the refrigerator or freezer until needed.

Yield: Pastry for 9-in (23-cm) double crust pie

STRAWBERRY
CUSTARD PIE

{ *A very pretty and delicious pie, this is a perfect complement to a summer afternoon tea. It looks as good as it tastes, and vice versa. If there is such a thing as a lady's pie, this would qualify — as delicate and feminine (and pink!) as can be. If you have a way of obtaining wild strawberries, they add a special intensity of flavour (if you live in the countryside send your children or grandchildren out to find some).* }

INGREDIENTS

Pastry for single crust 9-in (23-cm) pie, use ½ recipe Tender
   Pastry (page 53)
1 ½ cup (375 mL) milk
2 eggs, lightly beaten
2 tbsp (30 mL) granulated sugar
2 cups (500 mL) large strawberries, sliced or chopped
1 cup (250 mL) heavy cream (35% mf), whipped

METHOD

Preheat oven to 425°F (220°C). Set aside a 9-in (23-cm) pie plate.

Roll out the crust on a lightly floured counter to a 12-in (30-cm) circle, then fit into the pie plate. Crimp the edges of the crust and then refrigerate for ½ hour, loosely covered in plastic.

Remove crust from refrigerator and prick with the tines of a fork, then line with aluminum foil. Fill with dried beans or pie weights. Bake for 10 to 12 minutes, then remove the foil with the weights. Bake for approximately 6 to 8 more minutes, until very pale golden, then remove to cool on a rack.

In the top of a double boiler, heat the milk just until it comes to a simmer.

In a bowl, beat the eggs and sugar together until light and foamy. Gradually pour in the scalded milk and stir well. Pour the mixture back into the top of the double boiler and heat on medium, stirring constantly until thickened. Evenly distribute 1 cup (250 mL) strawberries over the bottom crust, then pour the custard over the strawberries. Bake for 40 minutes until knife inserted near edge comes out clean.

Once cooled, spread the whipped cream on top of the pie and decoratively arrange the remaining 1 cup (250 mL) of strawberries on top.

Yield: 8 servings

LEMON BUTTER
TARTS

{ *Lemon butter is more widely known as lemon curd, and less known as lemon cheese. It's a nicely slippery, jiggly, intensely tart/sweet confection that can be used in place of icing between cake layers, or instead of jam on a piece of toast. Most classically, it is a filling for pies and tarts! Your kitchen will seem sunnier with this fragrance emanating from the pot on your stove.* }

INGREDIENTS

Pastry for single crust 9-in (23-cm) pie, use ½ recipe Tender
   Pastry (page 53)
2 tsp (10 mL) grated lemon zest
½ cup (125 mL) freshly squeezed lemon juice
1 ½ cups (375 mL) granulated sugar
3 eggs
½ cup (125 mL) butter, diced
Whipped cream to serve (optional)

METHOD

Preheat oven to 425°F (220°C). Set aside 8 3-in (8-cm) tart plates.

Cut the pie dough into 8 pieces, then gently form each into a ball, wrap in plastic wrap and place in the refrigerator to chill.

Working with one ball at a time, keeping the rest in the refrigerator, roll each ball out individually on a lightly floured counter to a 6-in (15-cm) circle, then fit into the tart plates. Crimp the edges of the crust and then refrigerate for ½ hour, loosely covered in plastic. Continue to roll out the tart dough and refrigerate each tart after forming.

Remove the crusts from the refrigerator, prick with the tines of a fork, then line with aluminum foil. Fill with dried beans or pie weights. Bake for 8 to 10 minutes, then remove the foil with the weights. Bake until the crusts are deep golden brown on the edges and lightly golden in the centre, 6 to 10 minutes more, then remove to cool on a rack.

Whisk together the lemon zest, juice, sugar and eggs in a large heavy saucepan. Place on the stove, and heat to medium-low. Stir in the butter and cook, whisking frequently, until the mixture is thick enough to show the marks of the whisk and it just comes to a light simmer, about 6 minutes. Remove the mixture from the heat immediately, then transfer it to a bowl, place plastic wrap directly onto the surface and chill for at least 1 hour.

Spoon the chilled lemon curd into the baked tart shells, top with the whipped cream, and serve.

Yield: 8 servings

NOVA SCOTIA
APPLE PIE

This makes a classic apple pie, and of course you should use traditional Nova Scotian apples — how about some Gravensteins, the variety that solidified the Annapolis Valley's reputation as an apple-growing region? A dollop of Homemade Vanilla Ice Cream (page 111) is the classic accompaniment, but you can always go the extra-sharp cheddar route, or have the pie all on its own.

INGREDIENTS

6 cups (1.5 L) Nova Scotia apples, peeled and cut into ¼-in (5-mm) slices
2 tbsp (30 mL) all-purpose flour
¾ cup (175 mL) granulated sugar (first amount)
½ tsp (2.5 mL) ground cinnamon
½ tsp (2.5 mL) ground nutmeg
Pinch of salt
Pastry for double crust 9-in (23-cm) pie, either Perfect Pastry (page 52) or Tender Pastry (page 53)
2 tbsp (30 mL) cold butter, diced
1 egg white, lightly beaten
1 tbsp (15 mL) granulated sugar (second amount)

METHOD

Preheat oven to 425°F (220°C). Set aside a 9-in (23-cm) pie plate. Place the sliced apples in a bowl.

In a smaller bowl, mix the flour, first amount of sugar, spices and salt. Add the flour mixture to the apples, reserving 2 tbsp (30 mL) of the mixture to add to bottom of pastry.

Roll out the bottom crust on a lightly floured counter to a 12-in (30-cm) circle, then fit into the pie plate, letting it hang over the edge. Roll out the top crust in the same way, and set aside.

Sprinkle the reserved flour mixture on the base of the bottom crust. Heap the apple mixture into the crust. Distribute the diced butter over the apples.

Lay the top crust over the apples, seal and crimp the edges and cut four vent holes in the top. Brush the crust with the egg white and then sprinkle with the second amount of sugar.

Bake at 425°F (220°C) for 25 minutes, then reduce to 375°F (190°C) and continue to bake until the crust is a deep golden brown, approximately 30 minutes longer.

Yield: 8 servings

WINDFALL
DESSERT PIE

This is an applesauce pie recipe. More closely resembling a custard pie, it is a very different textural experience from the classic sliced apple pie. It is an old recipe and I suspect a pragmatic one: not only is it delicious, but it is a good way of using older apples or windfalls. Once they're transformed into sauce, textural issues disappear! The nutmeg adds a distinctive hint of warm spiciness.

INGREDIENTS

8 cups (2 L) Nova Scotian apples, peeled and chopped (a good use of older apples)

2 cups (500 mL) water

1 tsp (5 mL) ground cinnamon

2 whole cloves

Grated rind of 2 lemons, divided

¾ cup (175 mL) granulated sugar

4 eggs, separated

½ cup (125 mL) butter, melted and cooled

1 lemon, juiced

2 tsp (10 mL) fresh ground nutmeg

Pastry for single crust 9-in (23-cm) pie, use ½ recipe Tender Pastry (page 53)

METHOD

Preheat oven to 375°F (190°C). Set aside a 9-in (23-cm) pie plate.

In a large pot, place the apples, water, cinnamon, cloves and the grated peel of 1 lemon. Cook on medium-low until the apples are quite soft. Stir in the sugar, remove the cloves and let cool slightly.

Purée the mixture in a food processor. Add the 4 egg yolks and 1 of the egg whites, the butter, the grated peel of the second lemon, the lemon juice and the nutmeg, then purée again until well combined and beaten.

Roll out the pie dough on a lightly floured counter to a 12-in (30-cm) circle, then fit into the pie plate, trimming and crimping the edge.

Pour the apple filling into the crust, then bake for ½ to 1 hour, until the filling is set.

Yield: 8 servings

RIBSTICKER
APPLE AND POTATO PIE

This pie has a very substantial filling, worthy of its name! As with the Carrot (and Potato) Steamed Pudding (page 94), it makes use of the most available foods. Traditionally in the winter there would be a lot of potatoes and apples laid by, so they naturally made their way into creatively adapted recipes from days gone by. As with all the recipes in this book, this one has been tested and updated for today's home cooks and tastes delicious!

INGREDIENTS

1 cup (250 mL) raw potatoes, grated
½ cup (125 mL) raisins
2 tbsp (30 mL) vinegar
½ cup (125 mL) brown sugar, packed
¾ tsp (4 mL) salt
¼ tsp (1 mL) ground nutmeg
½ cup (125 mL) raw apples, grated
2 tbsp (30 mL) molasses
1 tbsp (15 mL) butter
2 tbsp (30 mL) mixed peel
½ tsp (2.5 mL) ground cinnamon
1 cup (250 mL) hot water
Pastry for double crust 9-in (23-cm) pie, either Perfect Pastry (page 52) or Tender Pastry (page 53)

METHOD

Preheat oven to 375°F (190°C). Set aside a 9-in (23-cm) pie plate.

Mix all the ingredients together in a large pot and simmer on medium-low heat slowly until the mixture is thick, stirring frequently to make sure that it doesn't burn. Allow to cool slightly.

Roll out the bottom crust on a lightly floured counter to a 12-in (30-cm) circle, then fit into the pie plate, letting it hang over the edge. Roll out the top crust in the same way, and set aside.

Pour the filling into the bottom crust. Lay the top crust over the filling, seal and crimp the edges and cut four vent holes in the top.

Bake for ½ to 1 hour, until the filling is set.

Yield: 8 servings

DEEP-DISH APPLE PIE
WITH CREAM

{ *A satisfyingly squishy deep-dish apple pie, with a lovely creamy sauce. This would be wonderful after a winter's day of outdoor activities like skating, skiing or shovelling – or indoor activities like reading and napping, let's be honest! Sturdy and delicious.* }

INGREDIENTS

6 tart apples, peeled and sliced thin
1 cup (250 mL) brown sugar, packed
2 tsp (10 mL) lemon juice, freshly squeezed
1 tsp (5 mL) grated lemon zest
½ tsp (2.5 mL) ground nutmeg
½ tsp (2.5 mL) ground cinnamon
½ tsp (2.5 mL) salt
1 tbsp (15 mL) butter, cubed
Pastry for single crust 9-in (23-cm) pie, use ½ recipe Tender
    Pastry (page 53)
½ cup (125 mL) heavy cream (35% mf)

METHOD

Preheat oven to 425°F (220°C). Butter a 10-in by 6-in by 2-in (25-cm by 15-cm by 5-cm) baking dish and set aside.

In a bowl, stir together the sliced apples, sugar, lemon juice and zest, spices and salt. Pour the mixture into the prepared baking dish. Distribute the butter over the mixture.

Roll out the pastry on a lightly floured counter to a 12-in (30-cm) rectangle. Lay the pastry over the apple mixture, and press it down over the edges of the dish. Using the tines of a fork, mark the pastry into 8 squares, making a slit in the centre of each square with a sharp knife.

Bake for 20 minutes, then reduce to 350°F (180°C) and continue to bake for 30 to 40 minutes longer, until the pastry is golden.

Remove the pie from the oven and pour heavy cream into each slit in the top of the pastry. Serve warm.

Yield: 8 servings

SUMMER
STRAWBERRY PIE

This is a fairly unadulterated strawberry pie and a classic summer dessert that would have been served at farmhouse tables across the province back in the day! The fresh strawberries retain their shape and colour and this makes for a very beautiful pie when cut – a slice of summer.

INGREDIENTS

Pastry for double crust 9-in (23-cm) pie, use Tender Pastry (page 53)
3 cups (750 mL) fresh strawberries, sliced
1 cup (250 mL) granulated sugar
⅛ tsp (½ mL) salt
1 tbsp (15 mL) cornstarch
1 tbsp (15 mL) butter, diced

METHOD

Preheat oven to 425°F (220°C). Set aside a 9-in (23 cm) pie plate.

Roll out the bottom crust on a lightly floured counter to a 12-in (30 cm) circle, then fit into the pie plate, letting it hang over the edge. Roll out the top crust in the same way, and set aside.

Place the sliced strawberries in a large bowl. Mix the sugar, salt and cornstarch together, and add to the strawberries. Stir well. Add the strawberry filling to the bottom crust. Dot the top of the filling with the butter.

Lay the top crust over the filling, seal and crimp the edges and cut four vent holes in the top.

Bake for 10 minutes, then reduce to 350°F (180°C) and bake for 30 minutes longer, until golden.

Yield: 8 servings

BLACKBERRY
BRAMBLE PIE

Blackberries are a great combination of sweetness with just a hint of astringency, and when perfectly ripe, seem to burst in the mouth. Take a day to pick blackberries from the plentiful bushes that grow all over Nova Scotia in the late summer. Even though they can exact a price in scratches to arms and hands, they are worth it! (They pair very well with local apples, too.) This is delicious served with Custard Sauce (page 122).

INGREDIENTS

Pastry for double crust 9-in (23-cm) pie, either Perfect Pastry
(page 52) or Tender Pastry (page 53)
3 cups (750 mL) fresh blackberries
1 cup (250 mL) granulated sugar
2 tbsp (30 mL) all-purpose flour
2 tbsp (30 mL) lemon juice, freshly squeezed
1/8 tsp (1/2 mL) salt
1 tbsp (15 mL) butter, diced

METHOD

Preheat oven to 425°F (220°C). Set aside a 9-in (23-cm) pie plate.

Roll out the bottom crust on a lightly floured counter to a 12-in (30-cm) circle, then fit into the pie plate, letting it hang over the edge. Roll out the top crust in the same way, and set aside.

In a bowl, mix the blackberries together with the sugar, flour, lemon juice and salt. Pour the blackberry mixture into the bottom crust. Dot the filling with the butter.

Lay the top crust over the filling, seal and crimp the edges and cut four vent holes in the top.

Bake for 10 minutes, then reduce to 375°F (190°C) and bake for 25 to 30 minutes longer, until golden brown.

Yield: 8 servings

ACADIAN LEMON
BUTTERMILK PIE

{ *In traditional recipes there are so many examples of pies and other desserts being made from whatever is available. This is essentially a buttermilk custard pie. Buttermilk would have been available each time people churned butter — it is the milk left behind after the intense churning process. It's usually only used as a component in baking now, where the flavour isn't the focus, but its tanginess adds complexity and moisture to cakes. In this recipe it holds centre stage, like a lighter version of a lemon pie!* }

INGREDIENTS

Crust

Pastry for single crust 9-in (23-cm) pie, use ½ recipe Tender Pastry (page 53)

Filling

½ cup (125 mL) chilled buttermilk (first amount)

1 cup (250 mL) granulated sugar

3 tbsp (45 mL) cornstarch

2 egg yolks

¼ tsp (1 mL) salt

½ tsp (2.5 mL) grated lemon zest

¼ cup (60 mL) lemon juice, freshly squeezed

1 cup (250 mL) chilled buttermilk (second amount)

1 ½ tbsp (22 mL) butter, diced

Meringue

2 egg whites

¼ cup (60 mL) granulated sugar

¼ tsp (1 mL) cream of tartar

METHOD

Preheat oven to 425°F (220°C). Set aside a 9-in (23-cm) pie plate.

Roll out the crust on a lightly floured counter to a 12-in (30-cm) circle, then fit into the pie plate. Crimp the edges of the crust and then refrigerate for ½ hour, loosely covered in plastic.

Remove the crust from the refrigerator, prick with the tines of a fork, then line with aluminum foil. Fill with dried beans or pie weights. Bake for 10 to 12 minutes, then remove the foil with the weights. Bake until the crust is deep golden brown on the edges and lightly golden in the centre, 10 to 12 minutes more, then remove to cool on a rack.

Reduce oven to 350°F (180°C).

In a bowl, whisk together the first amount of chilled buttermilk, sugar and cornstarch.

In a smaller bowl, beat the egg yolks, then add the salt, lemon zest and lemon juice and stir together.

In a heavy pot on medium-high heat, bring the second amount buttermilk to a boil. Add the sugar mixture to the boiling buttermilk and cook, stirring constantly, until it is smooth. Pour the lemon mixture into the hot buttermilk mixture, then add the butter. Continue to cook for 2 minutes, stirring vigorously so that it doesn't curdle. Remove from heat and let cool for a few minutes, and then pour into the baked pie crust.

In a bowl, whip the egg whites and the ¼ cup (60 mL) sugar together with a handheld electric mixer until they form soft peaks. Add the cream of tartar and continue to whip on medium high speed until stiff peaks are formed. Spread the meringue evenly over the pie filling, covering the entire surface. Using an offset spatula or butter knife, make swirls and peaks in the meringue (this will add visual interest and lots of tasty caramelized bits!).

Place in the oven for approximately 20 minutes, until the meringue is nicely browned and caramelized. Cool, cut and serve.

Yield: 8 servings

RHUBARB
CLOUD PIE

{ *This is a wonderful combination of textures and flavours. The tartness and softness of local rhubarb is balanced by the sweetness and fluffiness of the meringue, with the added delight of the caramelization from the oven. This is a recipe that can come together quite quickly at the right time of year. If you keep rhubarb in your garden, you'll find it thrives in the Nova Scotia climate and comes back year after year with little care or attention. This is a fabulous spring recipe to make the most of the freshly sprouting stalks.* }

INGREDIENTS

Crust
Pastry for single crust 9-in (23-cm) pie, use ½ recipe Tender
   Pastry (page 53)

Filling
3 cups (750 mL) rhubarb, chopped
2 tbsp (30 mL) all-purpose flour
1 cup (250 mL) granulated sugar
Pinch of salt
3 egg yolks
1 cup (250 mL) light cream (12% mf)

Meringue
3 egg whites
¼ cup (60 mL) granulated sugar
¼ tsp (1 mL) cream of tartar

METHOD

Preheat oven to 375°F (190°C). Set aside a 9-in (23-cm) pie plate.

   Roll out the bottom crust on a lightly floured counter to a 12-in (30-cm) circle, then fit into the pie plate, crimping the edges.

   Place the chopped rhubarb into the pie crust. Whisk together the flour, 1 cup (250 mL) of the sugar, the salt, egg yolks and cream. Pour this mixture on top of the rhubarb.

   Bake for 50 to 60 minutes, until the pie crust is browned and the filling is set. Remove from the oven.

   While the pie cools slightly, place the egg whites in a bowl. Using a handheld electric mixer, beat the whites until they form soft peaks, then add the ¼ cup (60 mL) sugar and the cream of tartar. Continue to beat until the egg whites form stiff peaks.

   Spread the meringue over the filling and return the pie to the oven and bake until the meringue is golden brown, around 10 more minutes. Serve slightly warm.

Yield: 8 servings

SPICED
BLUEBERRY PIE

A simply classic recipe — the warmth of the spices and the tartness of the lemon zest further brighten the flavour of the pleasing blueberries. If you go blueberry picking, get as many buckets as you can, and freeze whatever's left over. Frozen blueberries also work well in the pie (but don't let them thaw first).

INGREDIENTS

Pastry for double crust 9-in (23-cm) pie, either Perfect Pastry (page 52) or Tender Pastry (page 53)

4 cups (1 L) blueberries

1 cup (250 mL) granulated sugar

2 tbsp (30 mL) all-purpose flour

¼ tsp (1 mL) ground cinnamon

⅛ tsp (½ mL) ground nutmeg

¼ tsp (1 mL) salt

2 tsp (10 mL) grated fresh lemon zest

2 tbsp (30 mL) butter, diced

METHOD

Preheat oven to 425°F (220°C). Set aside a 9-in (23-cm) pie plate.

Roll out the bottom crust on a lightly floured counter to a 12-in (30-cm) circle, then fit into the pie plate, letting it hang over the edge. Roll out the top crust in the same way, and set aside.

In a bowl, mix together the blueberries with the sugar, flour, spices, salt and lemon zest. Pour the berry mixture into the bottom crust. Dot the berry mixture with the butter.

Lay the top crust over the filling, seal and crimp the edges and cut four vent holes in the top.

Bake for 10 minutes, then reduce to 375°F (190°C) and bake for 25 to 30 minutes longer, until golden brown.

Yield: 8 servings

PUMPKIN PIE
WITH WHIPPED CREAM

One of my absolute favourite pies is one of the strangest, in a way. When people think of pumpkin in most cultures, it is used for savoury dishes, not sweet. But North America is a different story! Out of necessity, it was used by the earliest settlers as a multi-purpose food, and ended up in preserves as well as pies and breads and soups. I love the vegetal earthiness of the scent of pumpkin mixed with the ethereal butter of the crust and aromatic spices!

INGREDIENTS

Pastry for single crust 9-in (23-cm) pie, use ½ recipe Tender Pastry (page 53)

1 cup (250 mL) puréed pumpkin (or squash)

½ cup (125 mL) brown sugar, packed

2 tbsp (30 mL) molasses

1 tbsp (15 mL) butter, melted

1 tbsp (15 mL) ground cinnamon

½ tsp (2.5 mL) ground ginger

1 tsp (5 mL) salt

2 eggs, lightly beaten

1 cup (250 mL) heavy cream (35% mf)

Whipped cream for serving

METHOD

Preheat oven to 425°F (220°C). Set aside a 9-in (23-cm) pie plate.

Roll out the bottom crust on a lightly floured counter to a 12-in (30-cm) circle, then fit into the pie plate. Crimp the edges of the crust and then refrigerate for ½ hour, loosely covered in plastic.

Remove the crust from the refrigerator, prick with the tines of a fork, then line with aluminum foil. Fill with dried beans or pie weights. Bake for 10 to 12 minutes, then remove the foil with the weights. Bake for approximately 6 to 8 more minutes, until very pale golden, then remove to cool on a rack.

In a bowl, stir together the pumpkin, sugar, molasses, butter, spices and salt. Beat the eggs into the mixture, then add the cream and mix thoroughly.

Pour into the partially baked pie crust and place in the oven. Bake for 10 minutes, then reduce the heat to 325°F (170°C), and continue to bake for 45 minutes, until set or a tester comes out clean.

Serve with whipped cream.

Yield: 8 servings

CRANBERRY
(OR FOXBERRY) LATTICE PIE

{ *Cranberries are a native berry, and one that settlers embraced after learning about them from Indigenous populations. Foxberries are another name for lingonberries, and these can be substituted for the cranberries if desired — though you'll probably have to pick them yourself, as they are not commonly found in grocery stores (find them on the barrens of Guysborough and Richmond counties). The lattice method for the pie crust can be used on any of the berry pies; it is wonderful to see the jewel-like colours peeking through!* }

INGREDIENTS

Pastry for double crust 9-in (23-cm) pie, either Perfect Pastry (page 52) or Tender Pastry (page 53)

4 cups (1 L) cranberries, chopped

1 ½ cups (375 mL) granulated sugar

2 tbsp (30 mL) all-purpose flour

¼ tsp (1 mL) salt

3 tbsp (45 mL) water

1 tbsp (15 mL) butter, melted

1 egg, lightly beaten

1 tbsp (15 mL) milk

METHOD

Preheat oven to 425°F (220°C). Set aside a 9-in (23-cm) pie plate.

Roll out the bottom crust on a lightly floured counter to a 12-in (30-cm) circle, then fit into the pie plate, letting it hang over the edge. Place in the refrigerator to chill while working on the top crust.

Roll out the top crust in the same way, and place it on a parchment-covered baking sheet in the refrigerator to chill for at least 30 minutes before preparing the lattice strips.

In a bowl, mix the chopped cranberries with the sugar, flour, salt, water and melted butter. Pour the mixture into the pie crust and set aside.

Remove the top crust from the refrigerator and, using a pizza cutter or sharp knife, cut the crust into even strips roughly ¾-inch (2-cm) wide. Lay half the strips horizontally over the pie, spaced apart, using the longer strips in the middle of the pie and shorter strips toward the edges.

Fold every other strip back on itself. Lay one of the remaining strips of pie crust vertically over the pie so that it lays across the unfolded horizontal strips. Snug it up against the folded strips. Unfold the horizontal strips so they lay over the vertical strip.

Fold the strips running under the vertical strip back over top. Lay another vertical strip of pie crust over the pie, snugging it up as closely as possible to the preceding vertical strip. Continue swapping the folded and unfolded horizontal strips and adding one new vertical strip each time. Continue until one half of the pie is completely latticed.

Lattice the second half of the pie following the same pattern. Use the longer strips of pie dough in the middle of the pie and save the shorter strips for the edges.

If the crust starts to soften too much while you're creating the lattice, put the whole pie and any remaining strips of dough in the fridge for about 15 minutes to chill and firm up before continuing.

Trim the edges with a sharp knife if needed, then roll them inwards toward the centre of the pie. Firmly crimp the edges to seal.

In a small bowl, whisk together the egg and milk, then brush over the top of the pie.

Bake for 15 minutes, then reduce to 350°F (180°C) and bake for another 30 minutes.

Yield: 8 servings

BRAS D'OR LAKES
LEMON PIE

Presumably this recipe hails from the Bras d'Or Lake area in central Cape Breton, but it can be enjoyed anywhere! It is a wonderful pie to have in the middle of winter, when the sunny, sharp flavour of the lemon shines through the cold. It also makes a nice counterpoint to the often heavier meals of winter. Of course, it's delightful in the summer at a tea party, and a slice of this, alongside a slice of strawberry pie, makes for a refreshing mouthful.

INGREDIENTS

Pastry for single crust 9-in (23-cm) pie, use ½ recipe Tender
  Pastry (page 53)
Meringue
1 cup (250 mL) granulated sugar
3 tbsp (45 mL) cornstarch
¼ tsp (1 mL) salt
1 lemon, zested and juiced
1 cup (250 mL) boiling water
3 egg yolks
1 tbsp (15 mL) butter

MERINGUE

3 egg whites
3 tbsp (45 mL) granulated sugar
¼ tsp (1 mL) cream of tartar

METHOD

Preheat oven to 425°F (220°C). Set aside a 9-in (23-cm) pie plate.

Roll out the crust on a lightly floured counter to a 12-in (30-cm) circle, then fit into the pie plate. Crimp the edges of the crust and then refrigerate for ½ hour, loosely covered in plastic.

Remove the crust from the refrigerator, prick with the tines of a fork, then line with aluminum foil. Fill with dried beans or pie weights. Bake for 10 to 12 minutes, then remove the foil with the weights. Bake until the crust is deep golden brown on the edges and lightly golden in the centre, 10 to 12 minutes more, then remove to cool on a rack.

In a medium saucepan, whisk together 1 cup (250 mL) of the sugar, the cornstarch and salt. Add the lemon juice and boiling water, then whisk to combine. Place the egg yolks in a bowl and set aside. Place the pan over medium heat, and whisk constantly until the mixture begins to form bubbles and thickens.

Temper the egg yolks by slowly adding half of the hot sugar mixture to the yolks while constantly whisking. Add the tempered yolks back to the saucepan and return to the heat. Bring the mixture to a simmer and cook, stirring constantly with a rubber spatula, for 1 minute. Remove from the heat and stir in the butter and lemon zest until completely melted and blended. Immediately pour the filling into the pie crust and cover with plastic wrap pressed directly against the surface of the filling. Refrigerate while you make the meringue.

Set the oven to broil, 500 °F (260°C). In a bowl, whip the egg whites and 3 tbsp (45 mL) sugar together with a handheld electric mixer until they form soft peaks. Add the cream of tartar and continue to whip on medium-high speed until stiff peaks are formed. Spread the meringue evenly over the pie filling, covering the entire surface. Using an offset spatula or butter knife, make swirls and peaks in the meringue (this will add visual interest and lots of tasty caramelized bits!).

Bake for 2 to 5 minutes, until the meringue is nicely browned and caramelized. Cool, cut and serve.

Yield: 8 servings

FRESH PEAR
PIE

I love pears and feel they're under-used in the realm of baked goods. Nova Scotia produces some delicious pears — most commonly Clapp and Bartlett varieties — and if you work with them at the right time, they have a lovely firm but giving texture, without graininess. This pie was a specialty of many farmhouses. It is similar to apple pie, insofar as the appearance is concerned, but the flavour is distinctly different. Enjoy!

INGREDIENTS

Pastry for double crust 9-in (23-cm) pie, either Perfect Pastry
  (page 52) or Tender Pastry (page 53)
5 cups (1.25 L) pears, sliced, peeled and cored
⅓ cup (75 mL) lemon juice, freshly squeezed
1 cup (250 mL) granulated sugar
1 tbsp (15 mL) cornstarch
1 tbsp (15 mL) butter, diced

METHOD

Preheat oven to 425°F (220°C). Set aside a 9-in (23-cm) pie plate.

Roll out the bottom crust on a lightly floured counter to a 12-in (30-cm) circle, then fit into the pie plate, letting it hang over the edge. Roll out the top crust in the same way, and set aside.

In a bowl, gently toss together the pears with the lemon juice, sugar and cornstarch. Mound the pear mixture into the bottom crust. Dot the filling with the butter.

Lay the top crust over the filling, seal and crimp the edges and cut four vent holes in the top.

Bake for 10 minutes, then reduce to 375°F (190°C) and bake another 25 to 30 minutes, until golden brown.

Yield: 8 servings

MINCEMEAT
TART

{ *This is a very formidable recipe for a classic mincemeat pie or individual tart — a Christmas tradition! The recipe indicates that you can use beef or venison, so if you know any hunters, this might be a nice trade — some of their venison for a couple jars of mincemeat. The scent of the spices and other ingredients is very appealing, and the essence of holiday cooking in many ways. There is nothing shy about this combination of scents. Make this well in advance of the holidays to give the mincemeat time to mellow and let the flavours develop.* }

INGREDIENTS

Crust
Pastry for single crust 9-in (23-cm) pie, use ½ recipe Tender Pastry (page 53)

Filling
5 cups (1.25 L) chopped cooked beef or venison
2 ½ cups (625 mL) minced suet
7 ½ cups (1.75 L) apples, chopped
3 cups (750 mL) apple cider or apple juice
½ cup (125 mL) vinegar
¾ cup candied citron peel
1 cup (250 mL) molasses
5 cups (1.25 L) granulated sugar
1 ½ cups (375 mL) raisins
1 ½ tbsp (22 mL) salt
1 tbsp (15 mL) ground mace
1 tbsp (15 mL) ground cinnamon
1 tbsp (15 mL) ground cloves
1 tbsp (15 mL) ground allspice
2 nutmegs, grated
3 cups (750 mL) water, if needed
1 tsp (5 mL) almond extract
2 tbsp (30 mL) lemon extract
1 ½ cups (375 mL) brandy
2 lemons, zested and juiced
2 oranges, zested and juiced

METHOD
Sterilize jars and set aside.

In a very large pot, combine the ingredients in the order given, up to and including the spices. Let simmer on medium-low heat for 1 ½ hours. It might be necessary to add water if the mixture gets too dry, so check the moistness level periodically.

Remove from the heat, and stir in the almond and lemon extracts, the brandy and the juice and zest of the lemons and oranges. Spoon the hot mincemeat into sterilized jars. As the mixture cools the suet will harden, creating a seal to help preserve the mincemeat.

To use it right away, preheat oven to 425°F (220°C). Roll out pastry on a floured work surface and line a 9-in (23-cm) pie plate or 12 individual tart molds.

Fill tarts or pie crust with filling and bake for 15 minutes, then reduce to 350°F (180°C) and bake for another 30 minutes.

Yield: 12 cups (3 L) of filling for 8–12 servings of pie or 12 tarts

SHOO-FLY
SUGAR PIE

This recipe is originally from the Pennsylvania Dutch, but it caught on all across North America for fairly obvious reasons, given the time period — the ingredients were highly traded and available in all the colonies. It originally contained no eggs, so was most likely primarily made in the winter, when chickens are uninterested in laying eggs. The "shoo-fly" part is self-explanatory: flies like molasses and you do NOT want them to land in your pie!

INGREDIENTS

Pastry for single crust 9-in (23-cm) pie, use ½ recipe Perfect Pastry (page 52) or Tender Pastry (page 53)

¾ cup (175 mL) all-purpose flour

½ cup (125 mL) brown sugar, packed

½ tsp (2.5 mL) ground cinnamon

⅛ tsp (½ mL) ground nutmeg

⅛ tsp (½ mL) ground ginger

⅛ tsp (½ mL) ground cloves

½ tsp (2.5 mL) salt

4 tbsp (60 mL) cold butter, cubed

½ cup (125 mL) molasses

1 ½ tsp (8 mL) baking soda

¾ cup (175 mL) boiling water

1 egg, lightly beaten

METHOD

Preheat oven to 350°F (180°C). Set aside a 9-in (23-cm) pie plate.

Roll out the pie dough on a lightly floured counter to a 12-in (30-cm) circle, then fit into the pie plate, trimming and crimping the edge.

In a bowl, whisk together the flour with the sugar, spices and salt. Using two knives or a pastry cutter, cut in the butter until it is incorporated and the mixture has lumps the size of peas. Separate out half of this mixture into another bowl and set it aside.

Pour the molasses over one half of the crumb mixture, and stir. In a measuring cup, add the baking soda to the boiling water — it should fizz dramatically! — then pour this into the molasses mixture. Beat in the egg, then pour this mixture into the pastry-lined pie plate.

Sprinkle the remaining crumb mixture evenly on top of the pie, then bake for approximately 30 minutes, until dark brown and firm but still jiggly. Let cool to room temperature before cutting and serving.

Yield: 8 servings

CARAMEL MAPLE
TEMPTATION PIE

This is a very elegant, pleasing, special occasion pie (due to the cost of maple syrup), and utterly irresistible. It is a deep, sophisticated, caramel confection with the heady scent and flavour of maple. It is excellent with a dollop of whipped cream or Homemade Vanilla Ice Cream (page 111). In the past, more families tapped their own maple trees and boiled their own syrup. Now we (generally) tap our grocery stores. If you get the chance, it's worth visiting a maple syrup farm to see the process in action and taste the fresh syrup.

INGREDIENTS

Pastry for single crust 9-in (23-cm) pie, use ½ recipe Perfect Pastry (page 52) or Tender Pastry (page 53)
¼ cup (60 mL) butter, room temperature
1 cup (250 mL) brown sugar, packed
1 cup (250 mL) maple syrup
½ cup (125 mL) milk
3 eggs, separated
Ground nutmeg to taste

METHOD

Preheat oven to 350°F (180°C). Set aside a 9-in (23-cm) pie plate.

Roll out the pie dough on a lightly floured counter to a 12-in (30-cm) circle, then fit into the pie plate, trimming and crimping the edge.

In a bowl, beat together the butter with the sugar and maple syrup. Beat in the milk and the 3 egg yolks.

In a separate bowl, using a handheld electric mixer, beat the egg whites on medium high until they form stiff peaks. Gently fold the egg whites into the sugar mixture.

Pour the mixture into the pastry-lined pie plate. Sprinkle with a pinch of nutmeg. Bake for approximately 40 minutes, or until firm. Remove, cool and serve.

Yield: 8 servings

MARLBORO
APPLE TART

This tart has a very long history — there are records for it as "Marlborough Pie" from English recipe books dating as far back as the 1600s. It must have made the long trip across the Atlantic and established itself in the colonies. It was highly adaptable, as it used whatever apples were available in the area. It was probably also a good way to deal with apples that were at the end of their use, during the late winter and early spring. It has a very light texture, somewhat like a chiffon pie, and is a nice alternative to the chunkier apple pies!

INGREDIENTS

Pastry for single crust 9-in (23-cm) pie, use ½ recipe
  Perfect Pastry (page 52) or Tender Pastry (page 53)
6 tart Nova Scotian apples, like Empires or Russets
  (or Granny Smiths if no Nova Scotian are available),
  peeled, cored and quartered
½ cup (125 mL) water
½ cup (125 mL) granulated sugar
½ cup (125 mL) melted butter
½ cup (125 mL) milk
1 lemon, juiced and zested
2 eggs, separated
Pinch of salt
1 tsp (5 mL) ground nutmeg

METHOD

Preheat oven to 350°F (180°C). Set aside a 9-in (23-cm) pie plate.

Roll out the bottom crust on a lightly floured counter to a 12-in (30-cm) circle, then fit into the pie plate. Crimp the edges of the crust and refrigerate for ½ hour, loosely covered in plastic.

Remove the crust from the refrigerator, prick with the tines of a fork, then with aluminum foil. Fill with dried beans or pie weights. Bake for 10 to 12 minutes, then remove the foil with the weights. Bake for approximately 6 to 8 more minutes, until very pale golden, then remove to cool on a rack.

In a pot, combine the apples with water, and cook on medium-low heat until tender. Place a sieve over a bowl, and force the apples through the sieve. Stir into the apple pulp the sugar, melted butter, milk, lemon juice and zest, egg yolks, salt and nutmeg.

In a separate bowl, using a handheld electric mixer, beat the egg whites on medium high until stiff, then gently fold into the applesauce mixture.

Pour the filling into the prepared pie crust, then bake for about 25 minutes, until the filling is set but not too brown.

Yield: 8 servings

BAKED CHEESE
AND NUTMEG TART

{ *This recipe dates from a time when curds were much more available, as people made their own cheese. It might be a fun rainy-day project to make cottage cheese with kids, just to show the process of milk turning into a solid, but you can simply use a full-fat cottage cheese from the grocery store. The recipe for Homemade Cottage Cheese is included, should the mood hit! This makes a delicate custardy pie with the distinctive and complementary scent and flavour of nutmeg.* }

INGREDIENTS

Pastry for single crust 9-in (23-cm) pie, use ½ recipe Perfect Pastry (page 52) or Tender Pastry (page 53)

1 cup (250 mL) cottage cheese, homemade (recipe below) or store bought

¾ cup (175 mL) milk

¾ cup (175 mL) granulated sugar

2 eggs, lightly beaten

1 tbsp (15 mL) butter, melted

¼ tsp (1 mL) vanilla extract

1 tsp (5 mL) cornstarch

1 tsp (5 mL) salt

¼ tsp (1 mL) ground nutmeg

METHOD

Preheat oven to 350°F (180°C). Set aside a 9-in (23-cm) pie plate.

Roll out the pie dough on a lightly floured counter to a 12-in (30-cm) circle, then fit into the pie plate, trimming and crimping the edge.

In a bowl, mix all of the ingredients together and beat well, until they are smoothly incorporated.

Pour the filling into the pastry-lined pie plate and bake for 40 minutes or until set in the middle.

Yield: 8 servings

HOMEMADE COTTAGE CHEESE

{ *Homemade cottage cheese is on another level from most of the kinds you can get at the grocery store, although they are perfectly acceptable (especially when simply a component for baked goods, such as the Baked Cheese and Nutmeg Tart above). This is a creamy, full-fat cheese, and it is lovely served on its own or with fresh fruit and black pepper.* }

INGREDIENTS

16 cups (4 L) milk

¾ cup (175 mL) white vinegar

¾ tsp (4 mL) salt

½ cup (125 mL) heavy cream (35% mf) or buttermilk

METHOD

In a large nonreactive (enamel is good) saucepan, heat the milk over medium heat. Heat to 120°F (49°C) on a candy thermometer. Remove from the heat and gently pour in the vinegar. Stir slowly for 1 to 2 minutes. The curd will separate from the whey. Cover and allow to sit at room temperature for 30 minutes.

Pour the mixture into a colander lined with a tea towel or cheesecloth and set aside to drain for 5 minutes. Gather up the edges of the cloth and rinse under cold water for 3 to 5 minutes or until the curd is completely cooled, making sure to squeeze and move the mixture the whole time.

Once cooled, squeeze very well to make the mixture is dry as possible and transfer to a bowl. Add the salt and stir to combine, breaking up the curd into bite-size pieces as you go. If ready to serve immediately, stir in the heavy cream or buttermilk. If not, transfer to a sealable container and place in the refrigerator. Add the heavy cream or buttermilk right before serving.

Yield: 2 cups (500 mL)

BANBURY FRUIT
AND NUT TURNOVERS

There are many forms to the family of Banbury tarts, and these ones present themselves as charming little turnovers or dumplings. You can think of them as sweet little Christmas gifts, wrapped in pastry instead of wrapping paper! Each turnover hides a delightful surprise of fruits, nuts and spices. Super cute on a holiday sweets tray, these little turnovers are a lighter, faster alternative to traditional mincemeat tarts.

INGREDIENTS

Pastry for single crust 9-in (23-cm) pie, use 1/2 recipe Perfect Pastry (page 52) or Tender Pastry (page 53)

2 tbsp (30 mL) lemon juice, freshly squeezed

1 cup (250 mL) raisins, chopped

3/4 cup (175 mL) apples, peeled, cored and finely chopped

2 tbsp (30 mL) walnuts, chopped

1 tbsp (15 mL) orange marmalade

1/3 cup (75 mL) granulated sugar

Pinch of salt

3/4 tsp (4 mL) ground cloves

1/4 tsp (1 mL) ground mace

1 1/2 tsp (8 mL) ground cinnamon

2 tbsp (30 mL) melted butter

1/4 cup (60 mL) milk

METHOD

Preheat oven to 400°F (200°C). Line a baking sheet with parchment paper and set aside.

Roll out the pie dough on a lightly floured counter to approximately a 12-in by 8-in (30-cm by 20-cm) rectangle, and cut into 12 1-in (2-cm) squares. Place the squares on the prepared baking sheet, allowing a couple of inches between them.

In a bowl, combine the lemon juice, raisins, apples, walnuts, orange marmalade, sugar, salt, spices and the melted better. Stir well.

Place 1 tbsp (15 mL) of the mixture on each square. Fold each square over like a handkerchief, into a triangle. Press the edges together with a fork, then prick the tops with the fork. Brush all the squares with the milk and bake for 20 minutes until golden.

Yield: 12 servings

DATE SHORTBREAD TARTS
WITH FUDGE FROSTING

{ *Originally named Crystal Cliffs Pork Pies, this recipe traditionally hails from Antigonish. You may be relieved to note that these do not actually include pork! An unusual recipe for a shortbread-like tart with a fruit filling and a rich, fudgy topping. These would be a conversation-worthy addition to a bake sale.* }

INGREDIENTS

Date Filling

2 ½ cups (625 mL) pitted dates, chopped
1 ½ cups (375 mL) water
1 tsp (5 mL) vanilla extract

Tarts

½ cup (125 mL) butter
3 tbsp (45 mL) icing sugar
1 cup (250 mL) all-purpose flour, sifted

Frosting

1 cup (250 mL) brown sugar
¼ cup (60 mL) heavy cream (35% mf)
2 tsp (10 mL) butter
1 tsp (5 mL) maple extract

METHOD

Prepare the date filling first. In a pot, combine the dates and water and bring to a boil on high heat. Reduce the heat to low and cook, stirring occasionally, until thick, around 8 to 10 minutes. Remove from heat and mix in the vanilla. Let the mixture cool to room temperature.

For the tarts, preheat oven to 350°F (180°C). Grease a 12-cup muffin tin and set aside.

In a bowl, cream together the butter and icing sugar until smooth, then mix in the flour.

Distribute the dough into the muffin tins and press down with fingers or the back of a spoon. Bake for around 15 minutes until delicately browned. Let cool in the pan for 10 minutes or so.

Using the base of a slender wooden spoon, indent the middle of each tart. Spoon the cooled date filling into each hole.

For the frosting, in a medium pot, boil the brown sugar and heavy cream together for 3 minutes. Immediately whisk in the butter, then let the mixture cool.

Beat until thick, then mix in the maple extract.

Frost the filled tarts with the fudge frosting, using a butter knife or angled spatula.

Yield: 12 tarts

Desserts

SWEET BLACK CHERRY
PUDDING

This recipe is typical of the Bear River area, the so-called "Switzerland of Nova Scotia" – famous for its Cherry Carnival, which has been happening every summer for more than 120 years! Although cherries are excellent right off the tree, sun-warmed and juicy, they are also wonderful in summer desserts. Make sure that you pit the cherries over a bowl to catch all their juice. This is good, messy, delicious fun.

INGREDIENTS

4 cups (1 L) sweet black cherries, pitted, with any juice saved
4 cups (1 L) water, or enough to cover the cherries
½ cup (125 mL) granulated sugar (first amount)
½ cup (125 mL) granulated sugar (second amount)
¼ cup (60 mL) butter
1 egg, lightly beaten
¾ cup (175 mL) all-purpose flour
¼ tsp (1 mL) salt
1½ tsp (8 mL) baking powder
⅓ cup (75 mL) milk
2 tsp (10 mL) vanilla extract
1 cup (250 mL) heavy cream (35% mf), whipped or ice cream

METHOD

Preheat oven to 350°F (180°C). Butter a 9-inch (23-cm) square baking pan or skillet and set aside.

In a large pot, place the cherries, their juice and enough water to cover the cherries, then mix in the first amount of sugar. Bring the mixture to a boil on medium-high heat.

While the cherries are heating up, prepare the topping. In a bowl, cream together the second amount of sugar and the butter until soft. Add the egg and beat well.

In another bowl, sift together the flour, salt and baking powder. Add the dry ingredients to the topping mixture, alternating with the milk, then add the vanilla extract.

Pour the hot cherry mixture into the prepared pan, then spoon the batter on top. Bake 55 to 60 minutes until a cake tester comes out clean. Serve with whipped cream or ice cream.

Yield: 8 servings

ANNAPOLIS VALLEY
APPLE PUDDING

McIntosh, Cortland, Spartan, Red Delicious, Gravenstein and Idared are just some of the 50 or so varieties of apples still grown in the Annapolis Valley. (Almost 1,000 varieties were grown in the early 1900s!) In the old cookbook from which this recipe was adapted, it mentions that this was chosen as a recipe that was "most typical of Nova Scotia" in a Canada-wide competition — no doubt because it makes full use of local apples. This is a wonderfully homey, substantial sort of apple cake, in the same realm as a cobbler.

INGREDIENTS

6 medium-sized tart Nova Scotian apples, like Empire or
   Idared (or Granny Smiths if no local apples are available),
   peeled and sliced
3 tbsp (45 mL) granulated sugar (first amount)
1 1/2 cups (375 mL) all-purpose flour
1 tbsp (15 mL) baking powder
1/2 tsp (2.5 mL) salt
1/4 cup (60 mL) butter, room temperature
3/4 cup (175 mL) granulated sugar (second amount)
1 egg, well beaten
3/4 cup (175 mL) milk
1 tbsp (15 mL) granulated sugar (third amount)
1 tsp (5 mL) ground cinnamon
1 cup (250 mL) heavy cream (35% mf), whipped

METHOD

Preheat oven to 350°F (180°C). Grease a 10-in by 6-in by 2-in (25-cm by 15-cm by 5-cm) baking dish.

Arrange the apples in the bottom of the baking dish and sprinkle with the first amount of sugar.

In a bowl, sift together the flour, baking powder and salt.

In another bowl, cream together the butter with the second amount of sugar, until fluffy. Beat the egg into the butter mixture. Add dry ingredients to the butter mixture, alternating with milk, folding in lightly after each addition. Pour this mixture over the apples.

In a small bowl, combine the third amount of sugar and the cinnamon, then sprinkle on top of the batter.

Bake for 40 to 50 minutes, until cake tester come out clean. Serve with whipped cream.

Yield: 12 servings

HALIFAX RAISIN PUDDING
WITH CARAMEL SAUCE

Another name for this dessert was Tory Pudding with Liberal Sauce and it was served at dinners during political conventions. It's delicious, and I've used its other name to avoid having to talk politics at dinner! Make sure to adhere by proportional representation, however, and give everyone a nice spoonful. During the baking the batter will rise to the top with a rich brown caramel sauce underneath.

INGREDIENTS

1 cup (250 mL) brown sugar, packed (first amount)
2 cups (500 mL) boiling water
1 tbsp (15 mL) butter
¼ tsp (1 mL) ground nutmeg
1 cup (250 mL) all-purpose flour
⅛ tsp (½ mL) salt
2 tsp (10 mL) baking powder
¾ cup (175 mL) brown sugar, packed (second amount)
½ cup (125 mL) milk
½ cup (125 mL) raisins

METHOD

Preheat oven to 350°F (180°C). Butter a 4-cup (1-L) casserole dish and set aside.

In a bowl, stir together the first amount of brown sugar, the boiling water, butter and nutmeg. Pour the mixture into the prepared casserole dish.

In another bowl, whisk together the flour, salt and baking powder, then stir in the second amount of brown sugar. Gently mix in the milk, and then fold in the raisins. Drop the batter by the tablespoon on top of the sauce in the casserole dish.

Bake until golden brown, about 30 minutes. Serve warm or cold.

Yield: 12 servings

SNOW PUDDING

The "snow" in Snow Pudding is a light frothy mix of the gelatin and lemon and egg whites — it resembles a light, cold scoop of snow, if snow also had the delightful tang of lemon juice. This is a perfect dish after a heavy meal in the cold weather, and extra refreshing in the summertime as an alternative to ice cream — it is essentially a sorbet. It has no dairy in it on its own too, so a good option for the lactose intolerant. Serve with Custard Sauce (page 122).

INGREDIENTS

1 tbsp (15 mL) gelatin
¼ cup (60 mL) cold water
1 cup (250 mL) boiling water
Pinch of salt
¾ cup (175 mL) granulated sugar
1 tsp (5 mL) grated lemon rind
¼ cup (60 mL) lemon juice, freshly squeezed
2 egg whites

METHOD

Grease a 4-cup (1-L) jelly mold and set aside.

In a small bowl, soak the gelatin in the cold water for 5 minutes. Add the gelatin mixture to the pot of boiling water and stir until dissolved. Add the salt, sugar, lemon rind and juice. Cool until quite thick then beat until frothy.

In a separate bowl, beat the egg whites with a handheld electric mixer until they form stiff peaks. Gently fold the egg whites into the gelatin mixture. Pour the mixture into the prepared mold and chill for two hours, or until set.

Yield: 12 servings

HONEYCOMB
CUSTARD DESSERT

{ *This is an old-fashioned recipe that turns up in a lot of home cooks' family recipe books. Chilled, light, custard-based desserts are making a bit of a resurgence lately in restaurants — maybe this one will too, and for home cooking! The texture of this pudding resembles honeycomb, thus the name. I'm sure that people were more familiar with honeycombs in the past, when more people kept bees.* }

INGREDIENTS

1 tbsp (15 mL) gelatin
1 cup (250 mL) milk (first amount)
2 cups (750 mL) milk (second amount)
1 cup (250 mL) granulated sugar
3 eggs, separated

METHOD

Butter a 4-cup (1-L) jelly mold and set aside.

Soak gelatin for 1 hour in the first amount of milk.

Put the second amount of milk in a pot over low heat. Stir in the sugar and gelatin milk until dissolved.

In a bowl, lightly beat the egg yolks, then add to the milk mixture. Stir well with a whisk, while bringing the mixture to a light simmer.

In another bowl, beat the egg whites with a handheld electric mixer until stiff peaks are formed. Add the gelatin mixture to the egg whites. Stir this together quickly, then pour into the mold and let set in the refrigerator for 2 hours until firm.

Yield: 12 servings

STRAWBERRY
SHORTCAKE

{ *One of the most anticipated parts of summer is the parade of local berries, including delightful strawberries, both wild and cultivated. This is a nice old-fashioned style of shortcake, where the shortcake is a big biscuit that is split and buttered, and topped with sweetened, crushed, fresh local strawberries and whipped cream. It is easiest to obtain cultivated strawberries, for this quantity, but if you happen to be able to use wild strawberries, they almost have the intensity of strawberry jam in flavour! My mom used to make shortcakes in this manner, so baking this took me right back in time. Best eaten slightly warm.* }

INGREDIENTS

4 cups (1 L) strawberries, sliced
¼ cup (60 mL) granulated sugar
2 cups (500 mL) all-purpose flour
1 tbsp + 1 tsp (20 mL) baking powder
½ tsp (2.5 mL) salt
1 tbsp (15 mL) granulated sugar
¾ cup (175 mL) milk
⅓ cup (75 mL) cold butter, cubed
1 cup (250 mL) heavy cream (35% mf), whipped (optional)

METHOD

Preheat oven to 375°F (190°C). Butter an 8-in (25-cm) cake pan and set aside.

In a bowl, combine the strawberries and sugar, crushing slightly with a spoon, and set aside to allow the juices to release.

In a bowl, whisk together the flour, baking powder, salt and sugar, then add milk gradually. Knead together lightly in the bowl, then turn out onto a lightly floured surface and divide into two parts. Pat and roll out the two pieces into two circles, roughly 8 in (25 cm) in diameter, then place them in the pan, one on top of the other, pressing to fit the pan.

Bake 12 minutes or until lightly golden, then turn out onto a plate. Split the large biscuit, then spread with butter.

Spoon the strawberries between and on top of shortcakes, slice and serve with a generous spoonful of whipped cream, if desired.

Yield: 6 servings

OAT
FORACH

This is a very unusual, but easy to prepare, dessert. Forach is a traditional Halloween treat for the Gaelic-speaking youngsters in Cape Breton — and for the adults, perhaps a nice alternative to leftover candy, and even better with a dram of whiskey. All three ingredients in this recipe are usually readily available, and can be quickly combined to prepare a delightful crunchy cloud to serve to visitors. In Scotland, a variation of this is called Cranachan.

INGREDIENTS

2 cups (500 mL) heavy cream (35% mf)
1 cup (250 mL) rolled oats
¼ cup (60 mL) granulated sugar, or to taste

METHOD

In a bowl, whip the cream to stiff peaks, then mix in the rolled oats and add sugar to taste. Serve immediately!

Yield: 4 servings

EVE'S APPLE PUDDING
WITH CUSTARD

{ *In the original recipe, it instructs you to heat the ingredients "without any flutter"! I took that to mean not to let the custard come to a boil. It's such a great word for "boil" that I might have to use the word "flutter" from here on in. This is a traditional British dish – tasty and homey – perfect in the late autumn when there are fresh apples from the trees and a filling dessert is welcome on a crisp night.* }

INGREDIENTS

Baked apples

6 apples, peeled, cored and finely chopped
³⁄₄ cup (175 mL) bread crumbs
1 tsp (5 mL) salt
1 tsp (5 mL) ground cloves
1 tsp (5 mL) grated nutmeg
1 cup (250 mL) raisins
¹⁄₄ cup (60 mL) butter, cut into small pieces

Custard

1 cup (250 mL) milk
6 eggs, lightly beaten
³⁄₄ cup (175 mL) granulated sugar
1 tsp (5 mL) vanilla extract

METHOD

Preheat oven to 350°F (180°C). Butter a large 10-cup (2.5 L) casserole dish and set aside.

In a bowl, stir together the apples, bread crumbs, salt and spices. Pour into the prepared dish, then scatter the raisins on top of the mixture. Distribute the butter on top and then bake for 30 minutes, until a tester comes out clean, with a few crumbs.

In a medium-sized pot on low heat, heat the milk to a simmer.

In a large bowl, whisk the eggs with the sugar, then gradually whisk in the warm milk. Pour the mixture back into the pot, and whisk constantly until thickened. Remove from heat, whisk in the vanilla extract and pour through a sieve into a bowl.

Serve by scooping the pudding into bowls and spooning the warm custard on top.

Yield: 12 servings

CARROT (AND POTATO)
STEAMED PUDDING

{ *This is a lighter type of steamed pudding, traditionally recommended as good for the eyes. This is a good recipe for the deep of winter, with its liberal use of root vegetables, which store well. Older recipes were much freer in their use of potatoes and carrots for desserts, but there's no reason why this can't be a tradition that continues. So many root vegetables have a natural sweetness and starchiness, they lean toward desserts as easily as savoury dishes. A more familiar contemporary example of this is the ever-popular carrot cake! Serve with Sunshine Sauce (page 122) or Custard Sauce (page 122).* }

INGREDIENTS

½ cup (175 mL) butter, softened
½ cup (175 mL) granulated sugar
2 eggs
1 tsp (5 mL) vanilla extract
1 cup (250 mL) raw potato, finely grated
1 cup (250 mL) raw carrot, finely grated
1 cup (250 mL) all-purpose flour
1 tsp (5 mL) baking powder
1 tsp (5 mL) baking soda
1 tsp (5 mL) salt
1 tsp (5 mL) ground cinnamon
½ tsp (2.5 mL) ground nutmeg
¼ tsp (1.25 mL) ground cloves
1 cup (250 mL) raisins
1 cup (250 mL) currants or chopped dates
Sunshine Sauce (page 122) or Custard Sauce (page 122), to serve

METHOD

Butter a 6-cup (1.4-L) steamed pudding mold and set aside. Cut two pieces of parchment paper in rounds to cover the opening of the mold. Place them together and butter on both sides and set aside.

In a bowl, cream together the butter and sugar until fluffy, then add in the eggs and vanilla and beat. Stir in the grated vegetables.

In another bowl, sift together the flour with the baking powder, baking soda, salt and spices. Stir the dry ingredients into the vegetable mixture, then stir in the raisins and currants (or dates, if using).

Pour into the prepared mold, cover with the prepared parchment paper and secure with rubber bands. Place the filled mold on a small rack in a large stockpot filled with a few inches of cold water and add more cold water until it comes halfway up the side of the mold. Bring to a boil, lower the heat to medium-low, cover and boil for 1 ¼ to 1 ½ hours, until firm. You may need to replace the boiling water over that time.

Remove from the pot and invert onto a plate to release from the mold. Serve with the sauce of your choice.

Yield: 8 to 12 servings

AUNT KITTIE'S
PLUM PUDDING

Plums used to just mean any dried fruit, so typically plum puddings contain a fair quantity of raisins. It was a tradition to go from house to house in the 12 days following Christmas eating plum pudding; the thought was that you would have happy months to match the number of homes in which you ate plum pudding. And — bonus — you would get to eat 12 distinct plum puddings! This can also be served with Sunshine Sauce (page 122).

INGREDIENTS

1 cup (250 mL) chopped suet
1 cup (250 mL) milk
1 cup (250 mL) molasses
1 cup (250 mL) raisins
3 1/2 cups (875 mL) all-purpose flour
1 tbsp (15 mL) baking powder
1/2 tsp (2.5 mL) salt
1 tsp (5 mL) ground cinnamon
1 tsp (5 mL) ground nutmeg
1/2 tsp (2.5 mL) ground cloves or ground ginger
Maple syrup or Sunshine Sauce (page 122), to serve

METHOD

Butter a 7 1/2-cup (1.75-L) steamed pudding mold and set aside. Cut two pieces of parchment paper in rounds to cover the opening of the mold. Place them together and butter on both sides and then set aside.

In a large bowl, mix together the suet, milk and molasses. Stir in the raisins.

In a separate bowl, whisk together the flour, baking powder, salt and spices. Stir the dry ingredients into the wet ingredients and mix well.

Pour into the prepared mold, and cover with the buttered parchment paper and secure with rubber bands. Place the filled mold on a small rack in a large stockpot filled with a few inches of cold water. Add more cold water until it comes halfway up the side of the mold. Bring to a boil, lower the heat to medium-low, cover and boil for 2 1/2 to 3 hours, until firm. You may need to replace the boiling water over that time.

Remove from the pot and invert onto a plate to release from the mold. Serve with maple syrup or Sunshine Sauce.

Yield: 8 to 12 servings

BAKED APPLE
DUMPLINGS

{ *Apple dumplings are a satisfying, comforting apple dessert, and a nice variation on the theme of the familiar apple pie. It's one way to use up the windfalls during apple-picking season in Nova Scotia. If you make a double quantity of the pastry dough, then you will have extra on hand in the freezer to use when the mood hits!* }

INGREDIENTS

6 large apples, peeled, cored and sliced thin
¼ cup (60 mL) granulated sugar
Pinch of salt
½ tsp (2.5 mL) ground cinnamon
½ tsp (2.5 mL) ground nutmeg
Pastry for single crust 9-in (23-cm) pie, use Perfect Pastry (page 52) or Tender Pastry (page 53)
Molasses Sauce (page 124), to serve

METHOD

Preheat the oven to 375°F (190°C). Butter a 9-in by 13-in (23-cm by 34-cm) baking dish and set aside.

In a bowl, stir together the apples with the sugar, salt and spices.

Roll out the pastry dough into a large rectangle, about ¼-in (5-mm) thick. Cut into 8 squares.

Spoon the apple filling evenly onto the centre of each of the squares of dough. With slightly wet fingertips, bring one corner of pastry square up to the top of the apple filing, then bring the opposite corner to the top and press together. Bring up the two remaining corners, and seal. Slightly pinch the dough at the sides to completely seal in the filling.

Place in the prepared baking dish, and bake until the dumplings are golden, around 50 minutes. Serve with Molasses Sauce.

Yield: 8 servings

BAKED CORNMEAL
SPICE PUDDING

{ *This dessert used to be called "Indian Pudding" because it used cornmeal, which was one of the many new-world ingredients that the Indigenous peoples were using long before the Europeans arrived. This is a nicely dense, gently spiced pudding, with a pleasing tooth from the cornmeal. It doesn't look especially pretty in the bowl, but one bite and you'll be hooked!* }

INGREDIENTS

¼ cup (60 mL) finely ground cornmeal

1 cup (250 mL) cold water

2 cups (500 mL) scalded milk (milk that has been brought to a boil and then removed from heat)

1 ½ tbsp (22 mL) butter

½ cup (125 mL) molasses

½ cup (125 mL) brown sugar, packed

2 eggs, beaten

½ tsp (2.5 mL) salt

½ tsp (2.5 mL) ground cinnamon

½ tsp (2.5 mL) ground ginger

1 cup (250 mL) cold milk

¼ cup (60 mL) raisins (optional)

1 cup (250 mL) heavy cream (35% mf), whipped, or Homemade Vanilla Ice Cream (page 111), to serve

METHOD

Preheat oven to 325°F (170°C). Butter a 9-inch (23-cm) square baking pan, and set aside.

In a bowl, stir the cornmeal into the cold water, add scalded milk and whisk together. Stir in the butter, molasses, brown sugar, eggs, salt, spices and raisins if you are using them. Pour the cold milk over the mixture, then pour into the prepared pan.

Bake for 2 ½ hours, or until firm. Allow to cool for half an hour before serving.

Serve with whipped cream or Homemade Vanilla Ice Cream.

Yield: 8 servings

BLUEBERRY
GRUNT

{ *This dessert is traditionally served in the summer, smack in the middle of blueberry season. You can find blueberry U-picks all across the province. The high-bush varieties are quick and easy to pick — it's easy to end up with bucket loads of fresh fruit. This dessert comes together very quickly, so it's a great one to make if you have extra berries that you want to share with friends and family. It is one of the fabulous panoply of ridiculously named fruit desserts found locally.* }

INGREDIENTS

4 cups (1 L) blueberries
½ cup (125 mL) granulated sugar (or to taste) (first amount)
½ cup (125 mL) water
2 cups (500 mL) all-purpose flour
1 tbsp (15 mL) + 1 tsp (5 mL) baking powder
½ tsp (2.5 mL) salt
1 tsp (5 mL) granulated sugar (second amount)
½ cup (125 mL) chilled butter, cut into pieces
½ cup (125 mL) milk
1 cup (250 mL) heavy cream (35% mf), whipped, or Homemade Vanilla Ice Cream (page 111), to serve

METHOD

Preheat oven to 400°F (200°C). Butter a 9-inch (23-cm) square baking pan, and set aside.

Mix the berries, first amount of sugar and water together in a large pot. Cover and boil until there is plenty of juice, around 10 minutes. While this is boiling, prepare the biscuit mixture.

In a bowl, sift together the flour, baking powder, salt and second amount of sugar. With two knives or a pastry cutter, blend in the butter, then gently stir in enough milk to make a soft biscuit dough.

Place the hot berry mixture into the baking pan, then drop the dough by tablespoons on top. Cover tightly with aluminum foil, place in the oven and bake for 15 minutes without peeking. Remove the foil and place back into the oven for 10 minutes, or until the biscuit topping is golden.

Serve with whipped cream or Homemade Vanilla Ice Cream.

Yield: 6 servings

STEAMED BLUEBERRY
PUDDING

The blueberries in this pudding become little jam-like gems, with their characteristic summery, almost floral scent. This treatment is less common than their usual appearance in muffins, pies and grunts or cobblers, so it makes a nice variation on the theme, if you have the time to make it.

INGREDIENTS

¼ cup (60 mL) butter
⅔ cup (160 mL) granulated sugar
1 egg, beaten well
1 cup (250 mL) milk
2 ¼ cups (550 mL) all-purpose flour
Pinch of salt
1 tbsp (15 mL) + 1 tsp (5 mL) baking powder
1 ½ cups (375 mL) blueberries
1 tsp (5 mL) vanilla extract
Homemade Vanilla Ice Cream (page 111) or Custard Sauce (page 122), to serve

METHOD

Butter a 4-cup (1-L) steamed pudding mold and set aside. Cut two pieces of parchment paper in rounds to cover the opening of the mold. Place them together and butter on both sides and then set aside.

In a bowl, cream together the butter and sugar until soft, then beat in the egg. Stir in the milk.

In another bowl, whisk together the flour, salt and baking powder. Gently combine the dry ingredients with the wet ingredients, then fold in the blueberries and the vanilla extract.

Pour into the prepared mold, cover with the prepared parchment paper and secure with rubber bands. Place the filled mold on a small rack in a large stockpot filled with a few inches of cold water and add more cold water until it comes halfway up the side of the mold. Bring to a boil, lower the heat to medium-low, cover and boil for 1 ½ hours, until firm. You may need to replace the boiling water over that time.

Remove from the mold. This steamed pudding tastes good served with Homemade Vanilla Ice Cream (page 111) or Custard Sauce (page 122).

Yield: 6 to 8 servings

RAISIN ROLL
WITH VANILLA SAUCE

The story of this dessert is that apparently one morning the owner of a famous inn in Yarmouth left for town and asked the cook to make something special for dessert – something they had never had before; as a result, she devised this recipe. Even if this is apocryphal, the result is a very tasty concoction. This is essentially the same as a jelly roll, but with raisins instead – almost a cakey fig newton!

INGREDIENTS

Dough

6 tbsp (90 mL) butter
1/4 cup (60 mL) granulated sugar
1 egg, lightly beaten
3/4 cup (175 mL) milk
2 cups (500 mL) all-purpose flour
1 tbsp + 1 tsp (20 mL) baking powder
1/2 tsp (2.5 mL) salt

Filling

2 3/4 cups (670 mL) raisins, puréed in food processor or blender
1/2 cup (125 mL) granulated sugar
1 lemon, rind grated and juiced

Sauce

2 eggs, separated
1/4 cup (60 mL) granulated sugar
Pinch of salt
2 tbsp (30 mL) granulated sugar
1 tsp (5 mL) vanilla extract

METHOD

Preheat oven to 375°F (190°C). Line a baking sheet with parchment paper and set aside.

To prepare the dough, in a bowl, cream together the butter and sugar until light and fluffy. Beat in the egg and milk until well combined. Stir in the flour, baking powder and salt. Roll the dough out into a large rectangle, 1/2-in to 3/4-in (12-mm to 20-mm) thick.

For the filling, in a separate bowl, mix together the pureed raisins with sugar and the juice and grated rind of the lemon.

Spread the filling evenly over the dough, leaving a 1/2-in (12-mm) space around the edge. Roll up from the long side and place on the baking sheet, seam side down. Bake for 30 minutes, or until very lightly golden.

While the rolls are baking, prepare the sauce. In another bowl, beat the 2 egg whites with a handheld electric mixer until they form stiff peaks, and then mix in 1/4 cup (60 mL) sugar.

In a separate bowl, beat the 2 egg yolks with a pinch of salt until pale yellow in colour. Add 2 tbsp (30 mL) of sugar, then stir in the vanilla extract. Pour the egg yolk mixture slowly into the beaten whites.

Cut the baked rolls into 12 slices and serve hot with the sauce spooned on top.

Yield: 12 servings

OLD-FASHIONED
JAM ROLL

This is a very pretty dessert, and relatively easy to prepare. Use whatever jam, jelly or filling that strikes your fancy. If you have access to homemade jam, it will elevate the cake even more! Local berry jams such as raspberry and blueberry work just as well as strawberry, as do peach or red currant jelly, or even lemon curd. (Cloudberry – or bakeapple – berries are found in the remote bogs of Cape Breton, the Eastern Shore and parts of the Western Shore. They make a distinctly Nova Scotia jam that would make a lovely addition to this dessert.)

INGREDIENTS

¾ cup (175 mL) cake and pastry flour, sifted

1 tsp (5 mL) baking powder

¼ tsp (1 mL) salt

4 eggs, room temperature

1 ¼ cups (300 mL) granulated sugar

1 tsp (5 mL) vanilla extract

1 cup (250 mL) icing sugar, for dusting the cake

1 cup (250 mL) local strawberry jam (or other berry jam or filling of your choice)

1 cup (250 mL) heavy cream (35% mf), whipped, or Custard Sauce (page 122), to serve

METHOD

Preheat oven to 400°F (200°C). Line a 15-in by 10-in by 1-in (38-cm by 25-cm by 2-cm) jelly-roll pan with parchment paper, and set aside.

In a bowl, sift together the flour, baking powder and salt.

In a separate bowl, beat eggs well, gradually beating in the sugar. Continue to beat egg mixture until it is thick, fluffy and lemon coloured. Gently fold in the flour mixture, then stir in the vanilla extract. Spoon batter into the prepared pan, and spread it out to evenly fill the pan.

Bake for about 12 minutes, until the cake springs back when gently pressed in the centre. Let the cake cool for about 2 minutes on a cooling rack, then loosen the sides with a spatula. Sift a layer of icing sugar over the surface of the cake and cover with a clean tea towel. Place a second cake pan over the towel and quickly invert the cake, removing the pan it was baked in. Peel off the parchment paper and dust this surface with icing sugar. Roll the cake up from the 10-inch side with the towel and let it cool completely (cooling it rolled sets its "memory" so the cake won't crack once filled).

Stir the strawberry jam to soften. Unroll the cake and spread an even layer of jam over the cake. Roll the cake back up again, and dust the top with icing sugar.

Ideal served with Custard Sauce or whipped cream.

Yield: 12 servings

MOLASSES
DUFF

{ *This is a fairly light variation of a fig pudding. Duff apparently used to refer to the cloth that one would wrap the dough in for steaming. Smaller than a duffle bag, but still full of treats! This again makes use of the molasses that was the ubiquitous sweetener for a couple of centuries, until mainly replaced by granulated sugar. In fact, molasses was so common, it was used in a wide variety of applications, including a way to keep beef jerky moist, and as an additive to mortar in brickworks. In this duff, though, its purpose is a robust and caramel-like sweetness.* }

INGREDIENTS

1 egg
2 tbsp (30 mL) granulated sugar
½ cup (125 mL) molasses
2 tbsp (30 mL) butter, melted and cooled slightly
1 ½ cups (375 mL) all-purpose flour, sifted
¼ tsp (1 mL) salt
1 tsp (5 mL) baking soda
½ cup (125 mL) boiling water
Boozy Sherry Sauce (page 123), to serve

METHOD

Butter a 4-cup (1-L) steamed pudding mold and set aside. Cut two pieces of parchment paper in rounds to cover the opening of the mold. Place them together and butter on both sides and then set aside.

In a bowl, beat the egg until light and lemon-coloured. Gradually beat in the sugar and molasses. Stir in the melted butter.

In a small bowl, whisk together the flour, salt and baking soda. Alternating with the boiling water, stir into the egg mixture.

Pour the batter into the prepared pudding mold, cover with the prepared parchment paper and secure with rubber bands. Place the filled mold on a small rack in a large stockpot filled with a few inches of cold water and add more cold water until it comes halfway up the side of the mold. Bring to a boil, lower the heat to medium-low, cover and boil for 1 ½ hours, until firm. You may need to replace the boiling water over that time.

Serve with Boozy Sherry Sauce.

Yield: 6 to 8 servings

BAKED CRANBERRY
APPLES

This is a delightful combination of two of Nova Scotia's favourite fruits – one introduced that has become big business and one native that has remained popular. This is a classic, simple preparation, very healthy and excellent for a weeknight dessert. The tartness of the cranberries is further emphasized by the orange zest. One of the most appealing aspects of this recipe is how quickly it comes together – it's one of the simplest recipes in the book!

INGREDIENTS

1 cup (250 mL) water (first amount)
1 cup (250 mL) granulated sugar
3 cups (750 mL) fresh or frozen cranberries
½ tsp (2.5 mL) freshly grated orange zest
6 firm apples, cored
1 cup (250 mL) water (second amount)

METHOD

Preheat oven to 350°F (180°C). Set aside a 10-in by 6-in by 2-in (25-cm by 15-cm by 5-cm) baking dish.

In a large pot, bring first amount of water and the sugar to a boil, stirring until sugar is dissolved. Add cranberries and simmer, stirring occasionally, until berries just pop, 10 to 12 minutes. Stir in the orange zest, then cool.

Starting at the stem end, pare apples one third of the way down. Arrange them in the baking dish with the pared sides up. Stir the second amount of water into the cranberry sauce and pour 2 cups (500 mL) of the sauce over the apples.

Bake for ½ to 1 hour, basting frequently until the apples are tender.

Yield: 6 servings

CRANBERRY
DUFF

{ *Cranberries are native to North America, and have always grown well in Nova Scotian bogs. They are refreshingly tangy and make for a lively addition to puddings as well as other baked goods. If you get a chance to participate in some cranberry picking in the autumn, I recommend it. The Terra Beata Farm near Lunenburg is my local cranberry U-pick and has a Bog Store that is open year round. In this recipe, the tartness is enlivened by a little bit of orange zest — not a local ingredient, but a fine complement. To make a "Raisin Duff," just substitute raisins for the cranberries, and omit the orange zest.* }

INGREDIENTS

2 cups (500 mL) all-purpose flour
½ cup (125 mL) granulated sugar
1 tsp (5 mL) salt
1 tbsp (15 mL) baking powder
½ cup (125 mL) chilled butter, cubed
1 cup (250 mL) fresh cranberries, chopped
2 tbsp (30 mL) grated orange zest
1 cup (250 mL) milk

METHOD

Butter a 4-cup (1-L) steamed pudding mold and set aside. Cut two pieces of parchment paper in rounds to cover the opening of the mold. Place them together and butter on both sides and then set aside.

In a bowl, stir together the flour, sugar, salt and baking powder. Using two knives or a pastry cutter, cut the butter into the dry mixture, until it is the texture of peas. Stir the cranberries and orange zest into the dough, then add the milk and stir until just combined.

Pour into the prepared mold, cover with the prepared parchment paper and secure with rubber bands. Place the filled mold on a small rack in a large stockpot filled with a few inches of cold water and add more cold water until it comes halfway up the side of the mold. Bring to a boil, lower the heat to medium-low, cover and boil for 1 ½ to 2 hours, until firm. You may need to replace the boiling water over that time.

Serve with cream or Custard Sauce (page 122).

Yield: 6 to 8 servings

LEVI'S APPLE
CRISP

I don't know who Levi is, but he would have to fight me for a piece of this old-fashioned apple crisp! This is a great way to use the wide variety of local apples. A fun thing to do would be a Levi's Apple Crisp Levee, with each one made with a different variety of apple. The variety in texture, tartness or sweetness would all be highlighted.

INGREDIENTS

6 medium-sized Nova Scotia apples, peeled, cored and sliced
3 tbsp (45 mL) granulated sugar
1 tsp (5 mL) ground cinnamon
½ cup (125 mL) all-purpose flour
½ cup (125 mL) rolled oats
¾ cup (175 mL) brown sugar, packed
½ tsp (2.5 mL) salt
½ cup (125 mL) cold butter, diced
Heavy cream (35% mf), to serve

METHOD

Preheat oven to 350°F (180°C). Butter a 10-in by 6-in by 2-in (25-cm by 15-cm by 5-cm) baking dish and set aside.

In a bowl, toss together the sliced apples with the sugar and cinnamon, then mound them into the prepared baking dish.

In another bowl, sift together the flour, rolled oats, brown sugar and salt. Using two butter knives or a pastry cutter, cut the butter into the dry mixture until it's incorporated and looks like large peas. Sprinkle the butter mixture over the apple mixture.

Bake for 40 minutes, until the topping is golden and the apple mixture is bubbling. Serve warm with the heavy cream poured on top of each serving.

Yield: 6 servings

HOMEMADE VANILLA
ICE CREAM

{ *This is the essential vanilla ice cream, which is custard based, and very smooth and voluptuous. Vanilla is the classic ice-cream flavour, and you can make it with a vanilla bean or vanilla extract. It is great made with just the vanilla extract, but if you can spring for the vanilla bean, it will add a wonderful dimension to the flavour (and you can rinse off the used vanilla bean and put it in some sugar to have some vanilla sugar for future use). In the past, ice-cream making was a real group effort, as hand-cranked ice cream took a lot of arm power (you can try your hand at churning ice cream the traditional way during the summer months at Ross Farm). It's a guarantee, though, that everyone will enjoy this dessert, and it is an excellent complement to many of the recipes in this book. There are a lot of very serviceable home ice-cream makers now. I use a canister that attaches to my stand mixer, and it produces consistent results.* }

INGREDIENTS

1 cup (250 mL) homogenized milk (3.25% mf)
¾ cup (175 mL) granulated sugar
1 cup (250 mL) heavy cream (35% mf) (first amount)
Pinch of salt
1 cup (250 mL) heavy cream (35% mf) (second amount)
6 large egg yolks
¾ tsp (4 mL) or 2 ½ tsp (12 mL) vanilla extract (depending on
   vanilla bean use)

Optional

1 vanilla bean, split lengthwise
1 cup (250 mL) fresh strawberries, blackberries or pitted
   cherries, mixed with ¼ cup (60 mL) granulated sugar, and
   crushed with a fork

METHOD

Warm the milk, sugar, first amount of the cream and salt in a medium pot. Scrape the seeds from the vanilla bean, if using, into the warm milk, and add the bean too. Cover the pot, remove from heat and let steep at room temperature for 30 minutes.

In a large bowl, pour the second amount of cream, and set a mesh strainer on top, then set aside.

In a separate medium bowl, thoroughly whisk the egg yolks until they are a pale yellow colour. Slowly pour the warm mixture into the egg yolks, whisking constantly (you might want a hand with this!), then pour this back into the pot.

Stir the mixture constantly over medium heat with a heatproof spatula or spoon, scraping the bottom while stirring, until the mixture thickens and coats the spatula. Immediately remove from the heat and pour the custard through the mesh strainer into the cream. Add the vanilla extract (¾ tsp [4 mL] if you used the vanilla bean or 2 ½ tsp [12 mL] if you didn't), and stir well, allowing to cool.

Chill the custard thoroughly in the refrigerator, 8 hours or overnight. When ready to churn, add in the crushed fruit mixture if using. Freeze the mixture in your ice-cream maker according to the manufacturer's instructions.

Yield: 4 cups (1 L)

AMARETTI TRIFLE
WITH SHERRY AND FRESH BERRIES

{ *This wild concoction is a traditional dessert to end a Christmas dinner, or for a Burns Night. It is boozy and rich, and the almond flavour is intensified if you use the amaretti together with the almond extract and toasted almonds. A fun, decadent showstopper! There is nothing retiring about this and in the spirit of Robbie Burns: "There's some are fou o' love divine;/There's some are fou o' brandy;/An' monie jobs that day begin,/May end in Houghmagandie/ Some ither day."* }

INGREDIENTS

½ recipe Classic Sponge Cake (page 30), cubed

2 eggs, lightly beaten

Pinch of salt

3 tbsp (45 mL) granulated sugar (first amount)

1 ½ cups (375 mL) milk

1 cup (250 mL) strawberry jam

6 store-bought amaretti biscuits, ladyfingers or macaroons, broken into crumbs

⅓ cup (75 mL) cream sherry

⅓ cup (75 mL) orange juice or fruit syrup

1 cup (250 mL) heavy cream (35% mf)

¼ cup (60 mL) granulated sugar (second amount)

1 tsp (5 mL) vanilla extract

½ tsp (2.5 mL) almond extract

2 tbsp (30 mL) toasted almonds, chopped

½ cup (125 mL) fresh raspberries or strawberries

METHOD

Set aside a large glass serving dish or bowl.

Make the custard: In the top part of a double boiler, whisk together the eggs, salt, first amount of sugar and the milk. Heat over medium-low heat, whisking constantly, until slightly thickened. Remove from heat and let cool.

Place the cubed sponge cake in the bottom of the serving dish. Stir the jam to loosen it, thinning slightly with some of the sherry if needed, then pour over the cake. Split the sponge layer in half horizontally and spread thickly with the jam. Sprinkle the crumbled cookies over the jam layer. In a small bowl, stir the sherry and the juice or syrup together, then pour over the cookie layer. Pour the cooled custard over the trifle. Cover and chill in the refrigerator for 8 hours or overnight.

Once chilled, use a handheld electric mixer to whip the cream with the second amount of sugar and vanilla and almond extracts, until it forms stiff peaks. Spread the whipped cream mixture over the chilled trifle.

Sprinkle with the chopped almonds, and decorate with the fresh berries when ready to serve.

Yield: 6 to 8 servings

GOOSEBERRY
FOOL

Gooseberries were imported to Nova Scotia by the British. They are less popular than such all-stars as blueberries and raspberries, but they have their own distinct pleasing qualities, including a refreshing tartness. The derivation of the word "fool" is obscure. It may have come from the French fol (mad), and perhaps refers to the fact that the fruit is all mixed up with sugar and cream. I love all the desserts with crazy names like "fool," "grunt," "mess" or "boy bait"! Whatever you call it, it's a simple, elegant dessert. (If gooseberries are unavailable, the best substitute would be a tart one like fresh cranberries, redcurrants or rhubarb.)

INGREDIENTS

3 cups (750 mL) fresh gooseberries, tops and tails trimmed, and
  halved lengthwise
½ cup (125 mL) granulated sugar (first amount)
1 cup (250 mL) heavy cream (35% mf)
¼ cup (60 mL) granulated sugar (second amount)

METHOD

In a heavy pot over medium heat, cook berries and first amount of sugar, stirring occasionally until liquid is thickened, about 5 minutes. Simmer mixture, mashing with a fork to a coarse purée, 2 minutes more. Chill purée, covered, until cold, about 1 hour and up to 1 day.

In a bowl, whip the heavy cream with the second amount of sugar, then fold in the purée carefully.

Pour into individual sherbet glasses or into a glass serving dish and chill, covered, for at least 3 hours.

Yield: 4 servings

EASY STEAMED
RHUBARB

This recipe comes from a famous South Shore Lodge. This is a really nice way to prepare fresh rhubarb, which is plentiful in Nova Scotia in the early spring — it is one of the first food plants harvested (and is actually a vegetable!). Steamed rhubarb maintains its integrity more than when it is stewed, so there will still be noticeable chunks in this preparation, rather than a homogenous purée.

INGREDIENTS

4 cups (1 L) rhubarb, cut in 1-in (2-cm) pieces
1 cup (250 mL) fruit sugar
Homemade Vanilla Ice Cream (page 111) or Custard Sauce (page 122),
  to serve

METHOD

In the top of a double boiler, place a layer of the chopped rhubarb. Add a layer of fruit sugar. Repeat layering the rhubarb and sugar until the rhubarb is finished, making sure that the last layer is sugar. Cover tightly and steam over medium heat till the sugar and rhubarb juice form a syrup, and the rhubarb is tender but unbroken, around 40 minutes.

Chill in the refrigerator for at least two hours, then serve with Homemade Vanilla Ice Cream or Custard Sauce.

GRANDMA'S
BROWN SUGAR FUDGE

{ *The old instructions for this recipe were more of a methodology than a detailed recipe – no measurements were given at all! It's not a bad lesson, because it teaches, paradoxically, to trust in one's instinct – a big part of the learned art of baking and confectionery. It also meant you wouldn't need a candy thermometer, but you would need a porch on which to cool the fudge. Also a grandma to teach you this in the first place! This reminds me a lot of "tablet," a British fudge, which is very straightforward, with a melting, crumbly texture. Truly delicious!* }

INGREDIENTS

4 cups (1 L) brown sugar, packed
1 ½ cup (375 mL) heavy cream (35% mf)
½ cup (125 mL) butter
½ tsp (2.5 mL) vanilla extract

METHOD

Line a 9-in (23-cm) square pan with parchment paper and set aside.

In a heavy-bottomed pot, place the brown sugar, cream and butter on medium heat. Stirring occasionally, let the sugar melt thoroughly. Put a candy thermometer in so that it is submerged but it doesn't touch the bottom of the pan. Bring the mixture to a boil, without stirring, until it reaches 235°F (118°C) on the candy thermometer (also known as the soft ball stage, because when you drop a small spoonful into cold water it forms a soft ball). Remove from heat and allow to cool to 110°F (43°C) with absolutely NO stirring, around 10 minutes.

Add the vanilla extract, then beat with a wooden spoon very vigorously until the mixture thickens and loses its glossy appearance, and takes on a creamy look. This will take around 5 to 10 minutes, and it will become more difficult as it thickens. Once it gets to that point, pour into the prepared pan and allow to cool thoroughly and set, at least a few hours or overnight.

Remove from the pan, using the parchment paper to help lift it, then cut into small squares. Place into an airtight tin, separated by waxed paper, and store at room temperature.

Yield: Approximately 2 cups (450 mL)

OLD-FASHIONED
MOLASSES CANDY

This is pulled in much the same way as the Nutty Molasses Pull Taffy (page 119), but it has a spongy texture in comparison, due to the addition of the baking soda. The addition of the cream and other types of sugar add an additional complexity to the flavour. Another fun one to do with family and friends, and excellent on a sweets platter at Christmas.

INGREDIENTS

1 cup (250 mL) granulated sugar
1 cup (250 mL) brown sugar, packed
1 cup (250 mL) molasses
½ cup (125 mL) heavy cream (35% mf)
¼ cup (60 mL) water
Pinch of salt
¼ cup (60 mL) butter
½ tsp (2.5 mL) baking soda
1 tsp (5 mL) vanilla extract

METHOD

Line a 15-in by 10-in by 1-in (38-cm by 25-cm by 2-cm) jelly-roll pan with parchment paper, and set aside. Butter the blades of cooking scissors and set aside. Grease a baking sheet and set aside, and keep the remaining butter handy for buttering hands for the taffy pull.

In a heavy saucepan, place the sugars, molasses, cream and water and turn the heat up to medium-low. Bring the mixture to a low boil for around 10 minutes, stirring often, until the mixture reaches 255°F (124°C) on a candy thermometer and forms a firm ball when dropped from tip of spoon in cold water.

Beat in the butter, baking soda and vanilla extract, then pour onto the buttered baking sheet. Let the candy cool enough to handle. With buttered fingers, pull the candy into a rope that's ½ in (12 mm) in diameter. Using the buttered scissors, cut the candy into small pieces, then place on the parchment-lined jelly roll pan.

Candies can be wrapped individually in waxed paper or candy wrappers, or placed in a tin, separated by waxed paper.

Yield: Approximately 2 cups (450 mL)

NUTTY MOLASSES
PULL TAFFY

{ *This is a time-honoured recipe, and it is definitely a fun group activity! It was a traditional ending to a sleigh ride, but you don't have to do that first in order to make this candy. It is wonderfully fun to see the transformation of the molasses and other ingredients into this taffy — truly alchemical. A big part of the fun of this recipe is the pulling! Get your family and friends together for this one so that everyone can pull the molasses taffy together.* }

INGREDIENTS

2 cups (500 mL) brown sugar, packed
1/8 tsp (1/2 mL) cream of tartar
1 cup (250 mL) molasses
2 tbsp (30 mL) butter
1 1/2 tsp (8 mL) white vinegar
1 tsp (5 mL) vanilla extract
1 cup (250 mL) chopped walnuts

METHOD

Line a 15-in by 10-in by 1-in (38-cm by 25-cm by 2-cm) jelly roll pan with parchment paper, and set aside. Butter the blades of cooking scissors and set aside. Butter a baking sheet and set aside, and keep the remaining butter handy for buttering hands for the taffy pull.

In a heavy saucepan, place the brown sugar over medium heat until it is melted. Add the cream of tartar, and bring to a low boil, stirring occasionally, for 15 minutes. Add the molasses and butter. Stir the mixture well and bring to the boiling point again. Boil for several minutes, stirring often, until the taffy reaches 255°F (124°C) on a candy thermometer and forms a firm ball when dropped from tip of spoon in cold water.

Working quickly, pour the taffy onto the buttered baking sheet. Add the vinegar, vanilla and nuts. With a knife or large spatula, fold over and over from each side, until the additional ingredients are well incorporated.

When cool enough to handle, using buttered fingers, pull the taffy until it is light-coloured. This is a good point to have all your family and friends join in! Form into strips and cut with buttered scissors into small pieces. You can either leave these in small smooth candy shapes, or twist them too. Arrange on the parchment-lined jelly roll pan to cool.

Pieces can be wrapped individually in waxed paper or candy wrappers, or put into a tin, separated by waxed paper.

Yield: Approximately 2 cups (450 mL)

SNOW MAPLE CARAMELS

Maple syrup has long been used by Indigenous people in North America. The first written accounts of maple sugaring are from the French in the late 1500s, having witnessed its transformation from sap to syrup by the Mi'kmaq. In the 1700s, production began in earnest in Canada, and now it's known as an iconic sweet staple. This is a special and classic treat, a soft maple candy that forms when the boiled sugar hits the fresh cold snow. It's a wonderfully fun thing to do with children, especially on a snow day!

INGREDIENTS

Freshly fallen clean snow, as much as needed

½ cup (125 mL) pure maple syrup

For Accompaniment

Fresh hot coffee, plain doughnuts and sour pickles

METHOD

Gather the snow, and pack it down in a 9-in (23-cm) pie pan. Place the pan outside (if it's cold!) or in the freezer.

In a large pot, boil the maple syrup until it reaches 235°F (118°C) on a candy thermometer (the soft ball stage).

Remove the pan from heat, then transfer to a measuring cup and carefully drizzle or spoon the boiled syrup onto the packed snow. The syrup will cool as soon as it is dropped onto the snow, and resemble taffy or soft caramel.

Remove the pieces of hardened sugar from the snow and eat them, alternating with the pickles, and bites of the doughnuts dipped in the coffee (if desired).

Yield: 4 servings

THREE-INGREDIENT CANDY

A classic, extremely simple confection, made from only three ingredients! Try making this with white vinegar and apple cider vinegar to compare the flavours. I prefer the apple cider vinegar version, as it has an additional fruity quality that works very well with the caramelized sugar flavour. This is another great lesson in chemistry for kids and formed in the same way as the two molasses candies!

INGREDIENTS

2 tbsp (30 mL) butter

2 cups (500 mL) granulated sugar

½ cup (125 mL) vinegar, white or apple cider

METHOD

Line a 15-in by 10-in by 1-in (38-cm by 25-cm by 2-cm) jelly-roll pan with parchment paper, and set aside. Butter the blades of cooking scissors and set aside. Butter a baking sheet and set aside, and keep the remaining butter handy for buttering hands for the taffy pull.

In a heavy-bottomed pot, melt the butter over medium heat, then add the sugar and vinegar. Bring to a low boil and stir constantly until the sugar is dissolved, then occasionally until the mixture reaches 255°F (124°C) on a candy thermometer and becomes brittle when dropped from tip of spoon in cold water.

Pour onto the buttered baking sheet. When cooled enough to handle, using buttered fingers, pull the taffy until it is light-coloured. This is a good point to have all your family and friends join in! Form into strips and cut with buttered scissors into small pieces. You can either leave these in small, smooth candy shapes, or twist them too. Arrange on the parchment-lined jelly-roll pan to cool.

Pieces can be wrapped individually in waxed paper or candy wrappers, or put into a tin, separated by waxed paper.

Yield: Approximately 1 cup (225 mL)

CUSTARD
SAUCE

Excellent with the Snow Pudding (page 88), Aunt Kittie's Plum Pudding (page 96), steamed puddings or with bread pudding. A classic old recipe, its creaminess is very satisfying — sort of like warm ice cream in flavour, with the roundness of the eggy milk and fullness of the vanilla.

INGREDIENTS

4 egg yolks
2 cups (500 mL) milk
½ cup (125 mL) granulated sugar
Pinch of salt
1 tsp (5 mL) vanilla extract

METHOD

Combine the egg yolks, milk, sugar and salt together in the top of a double boiler. Cook on a low heat until the mixture thickens, stirring constantly.

Allow to cool slightly, then stir in the vanilla. Serve while warm!

Yield: 1 ½ cups (375 mL)

SUNSHINE
SAUCE

This is a whipped vanilla sauce made with raw eggs. It is a sweet, smooth counterpoint to the heavier desserts in this collection. Because of the raw egg, discard any leftover sauce as it doesn't keep.

INGREDIENTS

2 eggs, separated
½ cup (125 mL) to 1 cup (250 mL) icing sugar
1 tsp (5 mL) vanilla extract
Pinch of salt

METHOD

In a bowl, beat the egg whites with a handheld electric mixer until they form stiff peaks, then beat in half the icing sugar.

In a separate bowl, beat the egg yolks until thick, adding remaining sugar gradually. Combine the egg whites and yolks together, and then stir in the vanilla extract and a pinch of salt, to taste.

Yield: ½ to ¾ cup

BOOZY
SHERRY SAUCE

*This is an excellent accompaniment to the Molasses Duff
(page 106) or any of the other puddings in the book! Boozy
and sweet, a winning combination.*

INGREDIENTS
2 egg yolks
⅛ tsp (½ mL) salt
1 cup (250 mL) icing sugar
2 tbsp (30 mL) sherry
1 cup (250 mL) heavy cream (35% mf)

METHOD
In a bowl, beat together the egg yolks and salt until thick and
lemon coloured, then gradually beat in the sugar and sherry.

  In another bowl, using a handheld electric mixer, beat the
heavy cream until it forms stiff peaks. Right before serving the
sauce and pudding, fold the whipped cream into the egg and
sherry mixture.

Yield: 1 cup (250 mL)

BROWN
SUGAR SAUCE

*This is essentially a caramel sauce and comes together
quickly as a topping to the Cranberry Duff (page 108) – a
welcome crown of sweetness to the gently tart duff.*

INGREDIENTS
1 cup (250 mL) brown sugar, packed
1 tbsp (15 mL) cornstarch
Pinch of salt
1 cup (250 mL) boiling water
1 tbsp (15 mL) butter

METHOD
In the top of a double boiler over medium heat, stir together the
sugar with the cornstarch and salt.

  Add the boiling water and cook, stirring constantly, until thick.
Add butter and stir until incorporated. Serve hot.

Yield: 1 cup (250 mL)

MOLASSES
SAUCE

A slightly deeper, heavier – dare I say strapping? – sweet sauce for the Cranberry Duff (page 108), this is another quick preparation.

INGREDIENTS

½ cup (125 mL) granulated sugar
½ cup (125 mL) molasses
1 tbsp (15 mL) cornstarch
Pinch of salt
1 cup (250 mL) boiling water
1 tbsp (15 mL) butter

METHOD

In the top of a double boiler over medium heat, stir together the sugar and molasses with the cornstarch and salt.

Add the boiling water and cook, stirring constantly, until thick. Add butter and stir until incorporated. Serve hot.

Yield: 1 cup (250 mL)

FLORA DORA
SAUCE

This sauce is apparently named after the show girls of the "gay nineties," meaning the 1890s rather than the 1990s. It is a light, frothy, white sauce. It makes a nice sauce for any of the pudding recipes in this cookbook. (Note that this recipe uses raw egg, so don't keep any leftover sauce.)

INGREDIENTS

1 egg, separated
¾ cup (175 mL) icing sugar
½ tsp (2.5 mL) vanilla extract
¾ cup (175 mL) heavy cream (35% mf)

METHOD

In a bowl, using a handheld electric mixer, beat the egg white until it forms stiff peaks. Gradually beat in the sugar.

In a separate bowl, beat the egg yolk until pale yellow, and stir into the egg white and sugar mixture.

In another bowl, using a handheld electric mixer, beat the heavy cream until it forms stiff peaks, then fold it into the mixture.

Yield: 1 cup (250 mL)

INDEX

Page numbers in italics denote photographs. In a list of page numbers, those in bold denote the main recipe.

Acadian Lemon Buttermilk Pie, 65
Acadians, 10, 65
alcohol, 33, 74, 112, 123
almonds, 33, 34, 41, 112
Amaretti Trifle with Sherry and Fresh Berries, 112, *113*
Annapolis Valley Apple Pudding, 86
Antigonish, 82
apples
    Annapolis Valley Apple Pudding, 86
    Baked Apple Dumplings, 97
    Baked Cranberry Apples, 107
    Cinnamon Apple Gingerbread, 38
    Deep-Dish Apple Pie with Cream, 62
    Eve's Apple Pudding with Custard, 93
    Levi's Apple Crisp, 110
    Marlboro Apple Tart, 78
    Nova Scotia Apple Pie, 58
    Ribsticker Apple and Potato Pie, 60
    Windfall Dessert Pie, 59
Aunt Kittie's Plum Pudding, 96, 122
Aunt Mary's Dark Fruit Cake, 33

Baked Apple Dumplings, 97
Baked Cheese and Nutmeg Tart, 79
Baked Cornmeal Spice Pudding, 98, *99*
Baked Cranberry Apples, 107, *108*
Banbury Fruit and Nut Turnovers, 80, *81*
bannock (Scottish), 48
Bear River, NS, 84
beef, 74
berries
    Amaretti Trifle with Sherry and Fresh Berries, 112
    Baked Cranberry Apples, 107
    Best Berry Muffins, 29
    Blackberry Bramble Pie, 64
    Blueberry Grunt, 100
    Cranberry Duff, 108
    Cranberry (or Foxberry) Lattice Pie, 70
    Gooseberry Fool, 114

Lemon Blueberry Cake, 43
Spiced Blueberry Pie, 68
Steamed Blueberry Pudding, 102
Strawberry Custard Pie, 54, *54*
Strawberry Shortcake, 90
Summer Strawberry Pie, 63
    see also individual berries
Best Berry Muffins, 29, *29*
Best Scottish Shortbread, 18
biscuits, 49, *49*
blackberries, 28, 64
Blackberry Bramble Pie, 64
blueberries, 28, 43, 68, 100, 102
Blueberry Grunt, 100, *101*
blueberry pie, 68
blueberry pudding, 102
Boiled Raisin Spice Cake, 40
Boozy Sherry Sauce, 106, **123**
Boularderie Acadian Cookie, 10, *11*
brandy, 33, 74
Bras D'or Lakes Lemon Pie, 72
breakfast cake, 46
Brown Sugar Sauce, 38, **123**
Burns Night, 112
buttermilk, 38, 46, 65, 79
butter tarts, 56, *57*
Buttery Shortbread Cookies, 19, *19*

cakes, 25–50
    Aunt Mary's Dark Fruit Cake, 33
    Best Berry Muffins, 29
    Boiled Raisin Spice Cake, 40
    Centennial Lemon Cake, 32
    Cinnamon Apple Gingerbread, 38
    Classic Doughnuts, 47
    Classic Sponge Cake, 30
    Dundee Fruit Cake, 34
    Government House Tea Biscuits, 49
    Hot Coffee Fruit Loaf, 41
    Lemon Blueberry Cake, 43
    Lunenburg Skillet Scones, 50
    Maple Walnut Cake, 42

Neighbourly Pound Cake, 26
Never Fail Pound Cake, 28
Scottish Scones, 48
Spiced Crumb Cake, 46
War Cake, 36
candies, 115–120
    Grandma's Brown Sugar Fudge, 116
    Nutty Molasses Pull Taffy, 119
    Old-Fashioned Molasses Candy, 118
    Snow Maple Caramels, 120
    Three-Ingredient Candy, 120
Cape Breton Island, NS, 10, 12, 21, 72, 92, 104
Cape Breton Long Johns, 13, *13*
caramel, 120, 123
Caramel Maple Temptation Pie, 76, *77*
carrots, 94
Carrot (and Potato) Steamed Pudding, 94, *95*
Centennial Lemon Cake, 32
cheese, cottage, 79
cheese tart, 79
cherries, 84
Cherry Carnival, 84
Christmas baking, 16, 19, 28, 36, 96, 112
Cinnamon Apple Gingerbread, 38, *39*
Classic Doughnuts, 47
Classic Sponge Cake, **30**, *31*, 112
cloudberries, 104
coffee, 41, 120
cookies, 9–24
    Best Scottish Shortbread, 18
    Boularderie Acadian Cookie, 10
    Buttery Shortbread Cookies, 19
    Cape Breton Long Johns, 13
    Fat Archies, 12
    Ingonish Oatcakes, 21
    Lemon Raisin Cookie Sandwich, 22
    Margaree Molasses Cookies, 15
    Molasses Crisps, 14
    Oatbread Crisps, 24
    Oat Crackers, 23
    Old-Fashioned Sugar Cookies, 16, 22

The Cooking of Joy (Grandma Joy), 7
cornmeal pudding, 98, *99*
cottage cheese, 79
crackers, 23
Cranachan, 92
cranberries, 70, 107, 108
Cranberry Duff, **108,** *109*, 123, 124
Cranberry (or Foxberry) Lattice Pie, 70, *71*
crumb cake, 46
crusts, pie, 52, 53
custards
    Acadian Lemon Buttermilk Pie, 65
    Baked Cheese and Nutmeg Tart, 79
    Custard Sauce, 122
    Eve's Apple Pudding with Custard, 93
    Homemade Vanilla Ice Cream, 111
    Honeycomb Custard Dessert, 89
    Strawberry Custard Pie, 54
Custard Sauce, 122

Date Shortbread Tarts with Fudge
    Frosting, 82
Deep-Dish Apple Pie with Cream, 62
desserts, 83–114
    Amaretti Trifle with Sherry and
    Fresh Berries, 112
    Annapolis Valley Apple Pudding, 86
    Aunt Kittie's Plum Pudding, 96
    Baked Apple Dumplings, 97
    Baked Cornmeal Spice Pudding,
    98, *99*
    Baked Cranberry Apples, 107
    Blueberry Grunt, 100
    Boozy Sherry Sauce, 106
    Carrot (and Potato) Steamed
    Pudding, 94
    Classic Sponge Cake, 112
    Cranberry Duff, **108**
    Easy Steamed Rhubarb, 114
    Eve's Apple Pudding with Custard, 93
    Gooseberry Fool, 114
    Halifax Raisin Pudding with Caramel
    Sauce, 87, *87*
    Homemade Vanilla Ice Cream, 98
    Honeycomb Custard Dessert, 89
    Levi's Apple Crisp, 110
    Molasses Duff, 106
    Oat Forach, 92

Old-Fashioned Jam Roll, 104
    Raisin Roll with Vanilla Sauce, 103
    Snow Pudding, 88
    Steamed Blueberry Pudding, 102
    Strawberry Shortcake, 90
    Sweet Black Cherry Pudding, 84
    Tory Pudding with Liberal Sauce, 87
doughnuts, *47,* 120
Dundee Fruit Cake, 34, *35*

Eastern Shore, NS, 104
Easy Steamed Rhubarb, 114
Eve's Apple Pudding with Custard, 93

Fat Archies, 12
Flora Dora Sauce, 124
foxberries (lingonberries), 70
Fresh Pear Pie, 73, *73*
fruit cakes, 33, 34, *35*
fruit loaf, 41
fudge, 116, *117*
Fudge Frosting, 82

gelatin, 88, 89
gingerbread, 38
ginger snap, 15
gluten-free, 23
gooseberries, 114
Gooseberry Fool, 114
Government House Tea Biscuits, 49, *49*
Grandma's Brown Sugar Fudge, 116, *117*

Halifax Raisin Pudding with Caramel
    Sauce, 87, *87*
Hilchey, Mrs. Florence M., 7
Homemade Cottage Cheese, 79
Homemade Vanilla Ice Cream, 58, 98,
    100, 102, **111,** 114
Honeycomb Custard Dessert, 89, *89*
Hot Coffee Fruit Loaf, 41

ice cream, 58, 98, 100, 102, **111,** 114
Indigenous Peoples, 8, 98, 120
Ingonish Oatcakes, 21, *21*

jam roll, 104
jams, 104, 112

ladyfingers, 112
lard, 21, 52, 53
Lemon Blueberry Cake, 43, *44*
Lemon Butter Tarts, 56, *57*
Lemon Raisin Cookie Sandwich, 22
lemons
    Acadian Lemon Buttermilk Pie, 65
    Bras d'Or Lakes Lemon Pie, 72
    Centennial Lemon Cake, 32
    Lemon Blueberry Cake, 43
    Lemon Butter Tarts, 56
    Lemon Raisin Cookie Sandwich, 22
Levi's Apple Crisp, 110
lingonberries (foxberries), 70
Lunenburg Skillet Scones, 50

maple syrup
    Caramel Maple Temptation Pie, 76
    Maple Walnut Cake, 42
    Snow Maple Caramels, 120
Maple Walnut Cake, 42, *43*
Margaree Molasses Cookies, 15, *15*
Marlboro Apple Tart, 78
meringue, 66, 72
Mincemeat Tart, 74
molasses
    Margaree Molasses Cookies, 15
    Molasses Crisps, 14
    Molasses Duff, 106
    Molasses Sauce, 97
    Nutty Molasses Pull Taffy, 119
    Old-Fashioned Molasses Candy, 118
Molasses Crisps, 14
Molasses Duff, **106,** 123
Molasses Sauce, 97, **124**
muffins, 29, *29*

Neighbourly Pound Cake, 26, *27*
Never Fail Pound Cake, 28
Nova Scotia Apple Pie, 58
Nutty Molasses Pull Taffy, 119

Oatbread Crisps, 24
Oat Crackers, 23
Oat Forach, 92, *92*
oats
    Ingonish Oatcakes, 21
    Levi's Apple Crisp, 110

Oatbread Crisps, 24
Oat Crackers, 23
Oat Forach, 92
Old-Fashioned Jam Roll, 104, *105*
Old-Fashioned Molasses Candy, 118
Old-Fashioned Sugar Cookies, **16,***17*, 22
oranges/marmalade/zest, 74, 80, 107, 108, 112

pears, 73
Perfect Pastry, 52
pickles, 120
pies, 51–82
    Acadian Lemon Buttermilk Pie, 65
    Baked Cheese and Nutmeg Tart, 79
    Banbury Fruit and Nut Turnovers, 80
    Blackberry Bramble Pie, 64
    Bras d'Or Lakes Lemon Pie, 72
    Caramel Maple Temptation Pie, 76
    Cranberry (or Foxberry) Lattice Pie, 70
    Date Shortbread Tarts with Fudge Frosting, 82
    Deep-Dish Apple Pie with Cream, 62
    Fresh Pear Pie, 73
    Lemon Butter Tarts, 56
    Marlboro Apple Tart, 78
    Mincemeat Tart, 74
    Nova Scotia Apple Pie, 58
    Perfect Pastry, 52
    Pumpkin Pie with Whipped Cream, 69
    Rhubarb Cloud Pie, 66
    Ribsticker Apple and Potato Pie, 60
    Shoo-fly Sugar Pie, 75
    Spiced Blueberry Pie, 68
    Summer Strawberry Pie, 63
    Tender Pastry, 53
    Windfall Dessert Pie, 59
plum puddings, 96, 122
potatoes, 60, 94
pound cakes, 26, *27*, 28, 32
pumpkin, 69
The Pumpkin (Whittier), 7
Pumpkin Pie with Whipped Cream, 69
quick breads, 29, 48

raisin pudding, 87, *87*
Raisin Roll with Vanilla Sauce, 103
raspberries, 28, 112
rhubarb, 66, 114
Rhubarb Cloud Pie, 66, *67*
Ribsticker Apple and Potato Pie, 60, *61*
Ross Farm, NS, 111

sauces, 121–125
    Boozy Sherry Sauce, 123
    Brown Sugar Sauce, 123
    Custard Sauce, 122
    Flora Dora Sauce, 124
    Molasses Sauce, 124
    Sunshine Sauce, 122
scones, 48, 49, 50
Scotland, 8, 20, 23, 34, 48, 50, 92, 112
Scottish Scones, 48
sherry, 112, 123
Shoo-fly Sugar Pie, 75
shortbread, 18, 82
shortcake, 90
snow, 120
Snow Maple Caramels, 120
Snow Pudding, 88, 122
South Shore, NS, 114
spice cakes, 40, 46
Spiced Blueberry Pie, 68
Spiced Crumb Cake, 46
sponge cakes, 30
Steamed Blueberry Pudding, 102
strawberries
    Amaretti Trifle with Sherry and Fresh Berries, 112
    Best Berry Muffins, 29
    with ice cream, 111
    Old-Fashioned Jam Roll, 104
    Strawberry Custard Pie, 54, *54*
    Strawberry Shortcake, 90
    Summer Strawberry Pie, 63
Strawberry Custard Pie, 54, *54*
Strawberry Shortcake, 90, *91*
streusel, 46
suet, 74, 96
sugar cookies, 16
sugar pie, 75
Summer Strawberry Pie, 63
Sunshine Sauce, 94, 96, **122**

Sweet Black Cherry Pudding, 84, *85*

tarts, 56, 74, 78, 79, 82
tea biscuits, 49, *49*
Tender Pastry, 53
Terra Beata Farm, NS, 108
Three-Ingredient Candy, 120
Tory Pudding with Liberal Sauce, 87
A Treasury of Nova Scotia Heirloom Recipes (Hilchey), 7
trifle, 112, *113*
turnovers, 80, *81*

vegetables, 60, 94
venison, 74

walnuts, 42, 80
War Cake, 36, *37*
wedding cakes, 33
Western Shore, NS, 104
Whittier, John Greenleaf, 7
Windfall Dessert Pie, 59
wine, red, 33

yeast, 47